4/00

When Government Was Good

When Government
Was Good

MEMORIES OF A LIFE
IN POLITICS

Henry S. Reuss

The University of Wisconsin Press

The University of Wisconsin Press
2537 Daniels Street
Madison, Wisconsin 53718

3 Henrietta Street
London WC2E 8LU, England

1   3   5   4   2

Printed in the United States of America

Library of Congress Cataloging-in-Publication Data
Reuss, Henry S.
When government was good : memories of a life
in politics / Henry S. Reuss.
200 pp.   cm.
Includes index.
ISBN 0-299-16190-0 (cloth: alk. paper)
1. Reuss, Henry S.   2. Legislators—United States—Biography.
3. United States. Congress. House—Biography.   4. United States—
Politics and government—1945-1989.   I. Title.
E840.8.R46R48   1999
328.73′092—dc21
[B]   98-48747

To the electors of Wisconsin, gratefully

Contents

Illustrations

Foreword

In his twenty-eight years in the House of Representatives, Henry Reuss was perhaps the best-informed member of that convocation and certainly one of the most influential. And he was a good friend of other members and especially those who also sought worthy legislative ends. If by anyone he was considered indifferent or adverse, it was by the special-interest lobbyists. For them Representative Reuss was a fellow you didn't much bother with.

It is good indeed that such a public figure should write his memoirs. But here again it is especially so for Reuss. A less purposeful, less intelligent, more conventional author would have begun at the beginning, told of his or her life year by year with special attention to those when something happened. Not Reuss. He does tell of the German origins of the Reuss family, his education, of wartime Washington, and military and European experience. (I especially rejoiced in his account of his service with the wartime Office of Price Administration where I was in charge of price control and he one of the most effective of lawyers. As a result of our efforts and those of others, the greatest of wars and war mobilizations left no memory of inflation.) Then back to Milwaukee, various political adventures and misadventures, and on to Congress. It is on the years in Congress that the author's different and effective editorial organization takes over. Henceforth not chronology but issues.

Reuss tells in literate detail of the things he sought as a member of Congress over the years; the sources of his concern; the legislation, which he most often wrote himself; the reshuffling of congressional committees to gain support and passage; and his shifts in committee membership and leadership to serve his purposes. Those purposes ranged from the environment, effectively and not surprisingly that of Wisconsin; high employment and low inflation; international economic relationships; constitutional questions; much more in Washington; and eventually the particular needs and rewards of his Milwaukee home.

What would have been a confusing admixture of legislative effort and action in any one year here comes through as the distinctive pursuit of pressing issues and goals, some of them spanning a legislative lifetime. It is an admirably clear account of each effort and repeatedly tells of a marked legislative accomplishment. Finally, there comes word of his well-earned but wonderfully well-occupied retirement.

Henry Reuss has been my lifelong friend. When invited to write this word of introduction, I soon found that what might to some seem a task was for me truly a pleasure. So it will be to all readers. No legislator has told in such compelling fashion of the problem, the wise solution, and how one person went about getting it.

JOHN KENNETH GALBRAITH

Preface

In my eighty-sixth year I sit on the front step of my nineteenth-century log cabin near Milwaukee. Before me lie the blue waters of North Lake, where I once fished for bass and walleyes in the summer, stalked the migrating redhead and goldeneye in the fall, skated on the ice in winter. Behind me stand the glacial moraines and kettle-holes, the white pine groves, the bur oak clearings.

Like a weary salmon who has struggled against the current to return to his birthplace, I reflect on my long round trip. I grew up in German American Milwaukee. Stirred by the Great Depression and by World War II, I decided on a life in politics. After early disappointment, I arrived in Congress and stayed there for twenty-eight years.

I witnessed at firsthand government when it was good, roughly from 1948 to 1968. That golden twenty-year period offered presidents willing to assume the responsibilities of leadership; Congresses that were generally civil, unbought, and constructive; a Supreme Court ready to interpret the Constitution for modern times.

It saw the birth of those two instruments that contained Soviet expansion and contributed to later Soviet collapse—the Marshall Plan and the North Atlantic Treaty Organization (NATO). It was the time of national responsibility for full employment without inflation, the dollar as a world currency and free trade as a world goal, a constructive condominium of Congress and the Federal Reserve over monetary policy, a growing concern for the nation's environment and for its cities, and a concerted drive for equality and human rights.

I was lucky to be a part of all this. Today I am saddened at our retreat from the golden age. As I write, the nation is bogged down in the Lewinsky scandal and the preparations for an impeachment. I discuss in Chapter 12 how some of this trauma might have been avoided.

I am optimistic enough to believe that, after our present agony passes,

Americans will hear voices that they know speak the truth. That will help us recapture government that is good.

Because a memoir is by definition self-centered, I now specially thank those whose work with me during my years in Congress helped make them joyous—among them, Andy Rice, Dick and Sarah Sykes, Frank Getlein, Rick Wing, Joe Sisk, Judy Frieder, Holly Staebler, Judith and Bill Buechner, Frank and Ruth Wallick, Sara and Don Robinson, Peggy Flynn, Jim Wieghart, Peter Robinson, Jamie Galbraith, Phineas Indritz, Mary Pepys, Mike Brady, Marylin Cooper, Bob Tehan, Helaine Blumenfeld, Manny Kroog, John Karlick, Mark Bisnow, Everard and Bernice Munsey, Paul Nelson, Don Anderson, Joanne Murphy, and Morvie Colby.

It was a great pleasure to work with my publisher, the University of Wisconsin Press, and its very able Scott Lenz, Mary Elizabeth Braun, Joan Strasbaugh, Elizabeth Steinberg, Allen Mueller, and Polly Kummel.

Part I

GETTING THERE
(1912–1955)

1

Growing Up German American
(1912–1936)

I was born in my parents' home on North 26th Street, Milwaukee, on Washington's Birthday, February 22, 1912. Sharing a birthday with the father of our country was always a big thing for me, a holiday celebrated separately and not merged, as now, with Lincoln's into Presidents' Day. If George Washington were to contemplate the government of his country in 1999, the two-hundredth anniversary of his death, I'm not sure that he would find it good.

My heritage is wholly German. This was once common, for Milwaukee, the "German Athens," shared with Cincinnati and St. Louis the boast of being America's most German city.

MY FOREBEARS

On my father's side the family Bible, in Martin Luther's translation into German, dates to Carl Christian Reuss, born 1743, "citizen and needlemaker of Stuttgart." The trade of needlemaker, carried on for several generations, required precision workmanship: the hot iron had to cut a proper eye in the needle, for a jagged edge would sever the thread.

Carl's grandson married the daughter of Christian Fernand, "citizen and buttonmaker," in 1832.[1] As the family Bible recounts, their five sons, following the failed revolution of 1848 against Prussia, "emigrated to America. Gustav, born May 31, 1834, arrived in New York with the Bremen ship Washington in September 1853. He started working for the bank of Marshall and Ilsley in Milwaukee, where he advanced to president."

This was my grandfather, who died in 1916. His son, my father, Gustav Adolph Reuss, was born in 1868, finished high school, began working at the bank, and became executive vice president. He was a gentle soul, more interested in his hobbies than in banking. On our living room wall was

3

painted the motto from *The Merchant of Venice:* "With mirth and laughter let old wrinkles come." My father played the piano splendidly, and his large collection of piano music is now in the Milwaukee Public Library. He collected stamps, specializing in Portugal and Romania. He was an avid forester who planted a stand of white pine in 1911 at North Lake that is ninety feet high today.

Among the mementos on exhibition for the 150th anniversary of the Marshall and Ilsley Bank—now Wisconsin's largest—in 1997 was a photograph of three generations of M&I Reusses. My bank connection, rather tenuous, was as a check sorter during my summer vacations from college and briefly in 1946–1947 as a director. I relinquished the directorship by mutual consent when I started my campaign for the Milwaukee mayoralty in 1947. Like most banks, the M&I is a conservative institution, and it was natural that we went our separate ways.

My father was thirty-nine when he married my mother, Paula Schoellkopf Reuss, in 1908. On her side were equally energetic German American pioneers, all from Kirchheim unter Teck, Württemberg, near Stuttgart. Her grandmother Augusta Vogel was perhaps Milwaukee's earliest feminist entrepreneur. She ran a brick kiln in the late 1840s, making the cream-colored bricks that gave Milwaukee its nickname of "Cream City." The Vogel males soon opened a tannery on the banks of the Menominee River in partnership with Guido Pfister. The Pfister and Vogel Tannery became the world's largest before World War I, with a branch in Northampton, England. But at the end of the war it was caught with a large oversupply of leather and a sudden dearth of soldiers in need of boots. Its buildings, mostly of Vogel brick, still cover large parts of the Menominee Valley.

Mother's father was Henry Schoellkopf, whose father had arrived in Buffalo in 1842, also from Kirchheim unter Teck, Württemberg. Before the nineteenth century's end the Schoellkopfs of Buffalo had successfully pioneered a tannery, a flour mill, the Niagara Falls electric power plant, and a coal-tar chemical dye plant to use the new electric power. In 1875 Henry married his distant cousin Emilie Vogel of Milwaukee; she was nineteen and he twenty-four, and they made their home in Buffalo.

When Henry Schoellkopf died young, in 1880, his widow (my grandmother) moved back to Milwaukee and married Rudolph Nunnemacher, a banker. He died in 1895 and she remained a widow. She lived for many years in a large Victorian home at 17th and Grand (now Wisconsin) Avenues. Our family joined her there shortly after my birth and stayed until 1920, when we moved to Maryland Avenue and Newberry Boulevard on the East Side. My only memory of 17th and Grand is of the third floor and its impressive collection of Oriental arms and armor, assembled by a world-traveling Nunnemacher relative in the 1890s. Grandmother Nunnemacher gave the 17th and Grand site to the Milwaukee Children's Hospital in the early 1920s. She died in 1949 at ninety-three. I remember her as tiny in size but a dynamo in spirit.

The Schoellkopfs and Vogels, remembering their German hometown of Kirchheim, in 1891 established a foundation there "to serve local poor people, regardless of their religious affiliation." They were also responsible for the construction of a memorial fountain in the Kirchheim town square that evoked their cascading Niagara.

The Germanic instincts of my ancestors went deep. One aspect was a penchant for reverse migration — American women would marry German men. My mother's sister Elsie Schoellkopf married Cai von Rumohr, a dashing military figure from the Baltic; my father's sister Alice Reuss married Stefan Langer, an engineer who taught for years at the Technische Hochschule at Aachen; my elder sister Emmie married Herbert Spiess, a banker from Frankfurt.

(As a result, my German relatives and I were on opposite sides in World War II, and the German connection interfered with my brief military career. Shortly after Pearl Harbor I was offered a commission by the top-secret Pentagon agency that has been credited with cracking the German military code; when notation of my German relatives appeared on my record, the offer was hastily withdrawn.)

My mother, Paula Schoellkopf Reuss (1878–1958), made the transition from her German immigrant heritage to modern womanhood. Doing what was almost unheard of in those days, she "went east" to Wellesley College. A disciple of Jane Addams of Chicago's Hull House, my mother wrote to her classmates a few years after college: "I have a sewing class, a housekeeping class and now I have a little Mother's Club, which I enjoy more than anything else. The first hour we are together we have an English class, as most of the mothers are German and are very anxious to learn English. Then we sew, read, and sing together."

Fifty years later, as I worked the precincts of Milwaukee looking for votes, I often ran into these dear mothers and their descendants, who had not forgotten my mother's settlement house. Incidentally, though a lifelong Republican, she never protested when I became a Democrat and supported me loyally. She enjoyed coming to Washington, to see Congress and the historic homes of Virginia.

My parents seem to have had no problem with their German ancestry during World War I. War propaganda identified our Germanic foe as the Hun; sauerkraut became "liberty cabbage"; little Schleisingerville in Washington County became (and remains) Slinger. But the Reusses, like most of the Forty-Eighters — those who left Germany after the unsuccessful revolution of 1848 — had long since become loyal Americans. One of my earliest memories, Armistice Day 1918, is of my parents' tying a tin can to our Locomobile to represent the fallen kaiser and parading triumphantly around Milwaukee's downtown.

The atmosphere of my family's home, however, was deeply German. Oil paintings by German romanticists—a storm at sea, a bibliophile in his library, an Alpine meadow white with edelweiss—covered the walls. Although they spoke German only in fragments, my parents staunchly supported the German repertory company and the German-oriented music of the Chicago Symphony under conductor Frederick Stock at the Pabst Theater. Our dinner table was rich, perhaps too rich by modern standards, with such dishes as Koenigsberger klops (ground veal, pork, and beef with capers), Rindfleisch (boiled beef), and Kartoffelsalat mit speck (potato salad with bacon).

Years later, when I was in Congress, I found my German American background socially congenial and politically positive. I regularly made the German American rounds, visiting the

> Restaurants—Mader's, John Ernst's, Fritz Gust's, Old Heidelberg
> Gymnasts at the Turnverein
> Literary crowd at Goethe Haus at the Milwaukee Public Library
> Free thinkers of the Freie Gemeinde at Jefferson Hall
> Choristers of the Liederkranz and the Liedertafel
> Politically progressive picnickers at Carl Schurz Park
> Donau Schwaben, descendants of the Swabians whom the Empress
>   Maria Theresa settled down the Danube in Hungary and Romania
> Lustige B'ua, happy Bavarian dancers in leather pants
> Tavern owned by Sepp' Unterrainer, the magnificent zither player, near
>   the Pabst Brewery
> Wonderful Usinger's sausage factory

Nor was I forgetful of Milwaukee's other ethnic groups—Poles, Slovaks, Slovenes, Bohemians, Italians, Danes, Romanians, Hungarians, Croats, Serbs, Greeks, Jews, African Americans, Latinos, Asians, Russians, Latvians, Lithuanians, Dutch, Belgians, Luxemburgers, Scotch, Irish, Welsh, English, Albanians, French Canadians. For each I kept a folder, listing local leaders, national heroes, favorite dishes, likes and dislikes, and a few scraps of the native language. I resisted the melting pot metaphor and preferred to keep America a mosaic.

My German American heritage played a part in my congressional life in Washington as well as in Milwaukee. Chapter 4 tells how I served President Kennedy as an adviser on German American concerns in the 1960 election and later in the formation of the German version of the Peace Corps. I had many German connections. I became a close friend of Willy Brandt's and Fritz Erler's, both pillars of the Social Democratic Party. It was at their party conference in Karlsruhe in 1964 that I gave the Kennedy memorial address. My friends included leading conservatives, like Walter Casper, the industrialist, and Ottmar Emminger, director of the Bundesbank. Over the years I took part in numerous conferences in the Federal Republic. In late 1964, right after LBJ's landslide victory over Barry Goldwater, Rep. John Brademas, Democrat of Indiana, and I went on a speaking tour of the German universities. At the universities of Berlin, Hamburg, Heidelberg, Bonn, and Munich we "interpreted" the 1964 elections. Fortunately, as it turned out, we rejected suggestions from our audiences that the Republican Party was finished.[2]

EDUCATION

I was exposed from the beginning to a truly splendid education. For kindergarten I was received by Holy Angels, a fine Catholic girls' school near our West Side home—not bad for a Protestant male and a tribute to the true catholicity of Holy Angels.

Next came Milwaukee's German-English Academy, under the birchrod pedagogy of Max Griebsch, the principal. The academy, founded in 1851 by Peter Engelman, aimed to provide schoolchildren with the rigorous education of the German Realschule. The school placed great emphasis on manual and physical training. In shop class I created several innovative tie racks, and in gym I disported myself on the parallel bars and the sawhorses.

Years later, in 1981, the owners of the academy's 1891 Late Picturesque building on North Broadway gave it up for destruction, although it had been placed on the National Register of Historic Places in 1977. The wrecker's ball was about to swing when a number of us banded together, bought it, and were able to complete a historic reconstruction. Today it is a successful office building, anchoring the new downtown development along North Broadway.

For high school I attended Milwaukee Country Day School under the redoubtable English public school headmaster A. Gledden Santer, a Brit from India. Country Day, with its Church of England prayers, its "body sports," and its Latin studies, marked the general de-Germanization of Milwaukee culture that occurred in the 1920s. My Country Day classmates, unlike my Teutonic pals at German-English Academy, were of English descent: Swallow, Carhart, Patton, James, Stevens. One, Brooks Stevens, became a lifelong friend. He never let his crippling childhood polio stand in his way or cloud his panache. He attained international fame as an industrial designer of trains, autos, and all sorts of consumer goods. In our eighties we both ended up as Fellows of the Wisconsin Academy of Arts, Sciences and Letters.

I wasn't good at sports, then or later, whether it was football, basketball, baseball, golf, tennis, fly fishing or wing shooting. My parents sent me to Richie Mitchell, of the great Milwaukee boxing family, to learn the manly art of self-defense, but my ring debut resulted in a technical knock-out in a matter of seconds.

If not sports, what about music? Here too my parents squandered their resources on piano, banjo, mandolin, trumpet, and flute lessons, all to no avail.

Failure in sports and music concentrated my competitive instinct in other directions, where I felt I had a chance. One was editing school pub-lications from fifth grade to law school. Another was a project I hatched with my best friend, Everett Hyman, also born on Washington's birth-day. We had just turned twelve and had become First Class Boy Scouts when we learned that advancement to Life Scout required at least three months, Star Scout another three, and Eagle still another three—a total of nine months. Why not do the whole thing in just nine months and thus be-come the youngest Eagle Scouts in the world? Everett and I embarked on a frenzy of knot tying, bridge building, and fire by friction. We finished in a dead heat and thus simultaneously became the Youngest Eagle Scouts in the World. Though the world failed to enroll us in its book of records, the race honed my competitive spirit. Everett—like my able congressional district manager, Dick Sykes, and my sweet eldest child, Christopher—all died of accidents in the cruel water.

For my higher education I was to follow in the footsteps of my late uncle Henry Schoellkopf, my mother's brother. He had died at thirty-two in 1913, shortly after I was born. He gave me my name and became something of a role model for me. A big handsome black-haired man, he played fullback on the victorious Cornell football team, was named to Walter Camp's All-American team, and returned as head football coach. Uncle Henry went on to Harvard Law School, started a law practice in Milwaukee, married my charming aunt, Bessie Murphy, and had just fathered a little daughter, Catherine, when he suddenly and inexplicably took his own life.

Henry's suicide was kept from me for many years, until I was told of it in a rough way when I was a freshman at Cornell. All this mystique made the news traumatic. Nowadays, medication could have prevented what was obviously a depression-induced suicide, and I could have been told the truth. The presence of my uncle Henry has been with me over the years.

So it was that I went to Cornell University in Ithaca, New York, and to Harvard Law school at Cambridge, Massachusetts. At Cornell I majored in history and government and began my fascination with public policy. I became editor of the *Cornell Daily Sun,* Ithaca's full-fledged morning news-paper, an Associated Press member, and a considerable power both on and off campus. Its editorial page during my editorship shows a modestly liberal bent in matters of civil liberties and human rights. But I have trouble explaining an editorial dug up years later by some mischief maker: a November 1932 piece urging voters to favor Herbert Hoover over Franklin D. Roosevelt. Granted, when I wrote it I wasn't old enough to vote, but my rationale—don't change horses in midstream—was not impressive.

When I arrived at Harvard Law School in September 1933, the New Deal was just hitting its stride. Because my grades placed me third in my class, I was elected at the end of my first year to the *Harvard Law Review.*

When it came time to elect officers for our final year on the *Law Review,* Graham Claytor of Roanoke, Virginia, and I were locked for many ballots in a dead heat for the top office of president. Toward dawn Graham emerged the victor and became a meticulous and dedicated president of the *Review.* Our friendship continued throughout his long and distinguished life. In the late 1970s, when he was President Jimmy Carter's secretary of transportation, we worked closely together in making possible the much-needed reorganization of the Chicago, Milwaukee, St. Paul, and Pacific Railroad.

My consolation prize in the *Law Review* election was the post of legislation editor. In 1936 Washington was busy churning out New Deal legislation that called out for critical analysis in the *Harvard Law Review*—and our articles explored in depth the National Recovery Act, Public Utility Holding Company Act, and Agricultural Adjustment Act.

My years at the law school contributed much to my outlook on life. The rigorous Socratic dialogue of the classroom and the moot court exercises of my law club, which was named for Oliver Wendell Holmes, Jr., taught me how to think for myself. At the same time, the most timely and interesting body of law on which we operated was the New Deal legislation. So it is no wonder that I emerged from law school, certainly not yet a liberal but sufficiently exposed to the new public law to grasp that reason would be needed to deal with it.

But the economic, political, and social life of our time had not yet been fully revealed to me. I had learned procedure without substance. My education, in a word, had been elitist, one open only to young people of privilege. No African Americans attended my elementary or high schools. The few friendships I formed with black youngsters were at Indian Mound Boy Scout Camp out at Silver Lake in Waukesha County. I did meet one black guest at home—Roland Hayes, the famous tenor, whom my parents had invited for dinner when he was in Milwaukee for a concert. But that was it. Elite education was racist—and sexist too: the so-called Big Six fraternities at Cornell, to one of which I belonged, looked down on Cornell's female students and forbade any "fraternizing" with them. I defied the ban, more from interest in my own civil liberties than in the women's civil rights, and was heartily paddled for it. Harvard Law was *both* racist and sexist: neither black nor female was visible in those days.

9

A final question is how a liberal-progressive Democratic member of Congress sprang from such a long line of conservative-industrial-financial Republicans. The answer requires some insights into my ancestors and me. My German American forebears differed from the robber barons of nineteenth-century America. My ancestors had been tempered by their experience as Forty-Eighters, refugees from the petty tyrannies of provincial Germany who had come to seek a better and freer life. For my part, my education had at least taught me how to think. Now I was to enter a larger classroom, a classroom that included depression and war.

2

Depression and War
(1936–1946)

THE LAW

Milwaukee, to which I returned after law school in 1936, was deep in depression. I was lucky to get a job with Quarles Spence and Quarles, one of the city's old-line firms, for $125 a month. And, following the course of least resistance, I mooched on the hospitality of my parents and lived at home.

Quarles Spence and Quarles was heavy on Rhodes scholars—Leroy Burlingame, a senior partner and Walter Cronkite look-alike; Jefferson Burrus, a rowing hero; and Arthur Larson, of Scandinavian ancestry from North Dakota, who became secretary of labor in the Eisenhower administration and still later a disillusioned Republican and dean of the Duke University Law School. (In 1942, when I was at the Office of Price Administration, I enticed Burrus and Larson to join me there, which they did, to the OPA's considerable benefit.)

At home in Milwaukee I immediately started learning more about life. My legal activities were those of any fledgling lawyer of the day—automobile negligence lawsuits, divorces, small business problems. I well remember my first courtroom appearance. A client reported that he had lost the sight of an eye through a corneal ulcer incurred as he carved carcasses at the Plankinton Packing Company. Some carcasses, he said, were those of cows suffering from undulant fever (also known as Malta fever, or spontaneous abortion). The problem was that a successful suit for compensation would require expert testimony from a physician stating that undulant fever could cause a corneal ulcer. The medical literature was blank on the subject, and my list of forensic physicians failed to produce anyone willing to testify. Then, fortunately, I remembered a newfound friend, Dr. Manfred Landsberg, who had recently arrived as a refugee from Hitler's Europe; he had had such a case in Vienna and would be willing to testify. On the day of the trial my office sent along one of the senior partners, Kenneth Grubb, later a U.S. district judge, to sit behind and monitor Reuss's first case. I warmed up my witness to establish that he was not just another professional court-house hack.

"State your name, doctor."

"Are you licensed to practice medicine, and is your license on file with the proper authorities?"

Then: "Doctor, is this your first appearance in an American court-room?"

While Dr. Landsberg was answering in the affirmative, I could hear Grubb stage-whispering behind me: "Doctor, you've got nothing on Reuss." Despite this, my client got his award.

I soon got to know the whole range of Milwaukee's lawyers, a welcome broadening for someone immured in a corporate law firm. There were attorneys from every ethnic group—Polish, German, Jewish, a world without end. I began to make friends with some of those on the opposite economic side—labor lawyers like David Previant of the Teamsters and Max Raskin of the United Auto Workers.

Some of us younger lawyers, weary of the establishment character of the traditional bar association, decided to form a Junior Bar Association. We then proceeded to annoy the traditional law firms by demanding that they cease using on their mastheads the names of partners long deceased, on the ground that such a practice deceived the public. Because the tribunal for such matters was the senior bar, the insurrection failed.

By 1939 the depression had deepened, and our private law practice was showing it. At that time the position of assistant Milwaukee County corporation counsel—the civil side of county law—became vacant, and the county held a civil service exam to fill it. I decided to try for the job and was successful. My two years at the Milwaukee Courthouse were formative in at least two ways: they put me under the guidance of one of my great mentors, Oliver O'Boyle, county corporation counsel and prototypical sharp-witted Irish American advocate, and they gave me hands-on insight into the social and economic problems that underlay the depression.

Perhaps because of the stolidity of my own Germanic background, I have always been attracted by the Celtic, bardic, druidic character of the Irish. My beloved high school pal was Tom Keogh, my college roommate John Norris, my wife, Margaret Magrath, and my old boss Ollie O'Boyle. O'Boyle and I developed a great friendship. He taught me courtroom psychology, quite a bit of ethics, and the pleasure of laughter. He always backed me up when I found myself in a tight spot.

Once a particularly venal court-appointed "alienist," as psychiatrists were then called, complained bitterly about a cross-examination I had subjected him to and asked that I consult my boss before I came to any conclusion about his probity. I did, and Ollie replied: "A panhandler!"

My duties as assistant corporation counsel involved representing the county in matters that dealt with two shipwrecked segments of society—the mentally ill and the unemployed. When someone sought release from the county insane asylum, I had to represent the county at the court hearing. I came away from this with two strong observations: that the line between those of us who are sane and those who are not is a narrow one, and that an Elizabethan lockup was not the most humane locale for treatment.

These two perfectly reasonable views became widely held thirty years later and led to the perfectly reasonable solution to close the asylums and instead treat the mentally ill in half-way houses and in community-based relationships. The states, which were paying for the mental asylums, jumped at the chance to close them. But unfortunately, neither federal, state, or local government nor private charity did much about supplying the local alternatives so desperately needed.

Thus, when in the 1980s I did some volunteer work in Mitch Snyder's homeless shelter in downtown Washington, D.C., I saw with sadness that a large percentage of the homeless were the mentally ill who had been left on the streets when the asylums closed. Surely the failure to follow through by creating better alternatives to the closed asylums was unforgivable.

As for the unemployed, they numbered about 25 percent of Wisconsin's workforce during the depression. The county corporation counsel got involved because each county was to provide relief to those who had acquired "legal settlement" within its borders. There was much jockeying between the counties about where an unemployed person actually lived, because that county was the one to pay for his relief. So I found myself driving all over the state, trying lawsuits to establish that "legal settlement" was somewhere other than Milwaukee County. Along with me rode my witness, the unemployed person.

Thus I had plenty of time for one-on-one explorations of the life of someone who had lost his job. It was a soul-destroying experience for my witnesses. They had suffered not only the trauma of being cast on the slag heap without means to support their family. Just as painful was the realization that they were no longer part of society, which counted a job as the key to membership.

I kept asking myself what could be done about depression and joblessness. The economy, after all, was created by humans. Unlike the stars, whose course we could not alter, supply and demand were things that people could act upon. My traveling companions did not know that the sad stories they were pouring into my ear would kindle a lifelong quest for ways to end involuntary unemployment.

The political scene in Wisconsin in the late 1930s was desolate, and I remained aloof. My first presidential vote, in 1936, was strongly for FDR. However, in 1940 I voted for Wendell Willkie. I was convinced that FDR, blocked by southern Democrats, had run out of steam and that George Washington's two-term tradition (later mistakenly embedded in our Constitution) had something to it. I believed that Willkie represented a new internationalist, socially moderate Republicanism that recalled Teddy Roosevelt. In Milwaukee Dan Hoan's two decades of populism-socialism in the mayor's office were almost over, and he was to be toppled by handsome young Carl Zeidler in 1940. In the governor's seat was Phil La Follette, unworthy son and brother of Old and Young Bob. Phil's star sank in 1938, when he tried to form a national Progressive Party with some suspicious resemblance to the totalitarian parties then on the rise in Europe. The stalwart Wisconsin Republicans were hopelessly Neanderthal. As for the Democrats, they lived with no other thought than to be on hand to pass out patronage. Altogether, it was not a great time to be involved in politics, and I wasn't.

PRELUDE TO WAR

While all was soporific on the Wisconsin front, Western Europe was shaking. Hitler, Mussolini, and a dozen other dictators bestrode most historic capitals of Europe. The great democracies of Britain and France were atrophied and feckless. What was America to do?

In Milwaukee a small but sizable band of American Nazis were proposing that the United States go the way of Germany. With brownshirts and swastikas they marched at Camp Hindenburg on the Milwaukee River. (At the end of the war, in 1945, I found out what had happened to some of them. In Frankfurt I ran into my old friend Capt. Deering Danielson, who with his cavalry reconnaissance troop was headquartered at a mountain castle a few miles away. Invited over for dinner at his mess, I learned that the little village at the foot of the mountain was peopled by some of the Camp Hindenburg folks, much crestfallen now that they were among the defeated. They had headed to the Reich just before the war with such high hopes.)

In Germanic Milwaukee before the war it seemed right to take a stand. Accordingly, I helped found the Milwaukee chapter of the Committee to Defend America by Aiding the Allies, an organization whose name pretty accurately stated its purpose. We'd meet at the Hotel Pfister every week to plan strategy on how to mold public opinion for the ultimate conflict we saw between Hitler and us.

In late 1940, with France overrun and the Battle of Britain not yet concluded, I decided to join in the preparations for war underway in Washington (I had a high draft number). New agencies were being formed, and one that appealed to me was soon to be called the Office of Price Administration. It was dedicated to the goal that the coming war, unlike all our previous wars, should be kept free of runaway inflation. At its head was Leon Henderson, a New Deal tiger. I became assistant general counsel of the OPA, helping to set price controls on all commodities and to ration scarce items like tires, red meat, and gasoline. A joyous company of dedicated young people staffed the OPA, and I made many lifelong friends, among them David Ginsburg, the general counsel and today a prominent Washington lawyer, as well as lawyers Carl Auerbach, Harold Leventhal, and Tom Harris, and price control chief John Kenneth Galbraith, the celebrated economist and my mentor over the years.

I also found my lifelong wife, Margaret. This happy conjunction occurred in the summer of 1942, when my aunt Tadie Lindsay from Winnetka, Illinois, wrote that her friends' charming daughter, just graduated from Bryn Mawr, had arrived in Washington to work at the OPA, and would I be kind enough to look her up? I was and immediately discovered her splendid amalgam of beauty and brains. I pressed my suit, screwed up my courage, proposed, was accepted. We were married on October 28, 1942, at old Christ Church, Alexandria, where Washington and Lee had worshiped. Because of wartime crowding, our ceremony was conducted in a corner of the church. A christening and a funeral were going on simultaneously in other corners. For three months, before I was called to the colors, we made our home in a little house on Franklin Street in Alexandria.

Getting married meant an end to my bachelor life in Washington, which had been vibrant. After my long hours at Temporary D, the OPA's headquarters, I shared housing and recreational facilities with a dozen other bachelors at a couple of remarkable homes in succession: Hockley, a Mount Vernon–like mansion overlooking the Potomac in Virginia, and Foxhall Road, the elaborate structure once occupied by Nevada's silver senator, Key Pittman. By pooling our resources, we happy twelve were able to live like kings, entertaining celebrities at mint julep parties and passing our evenings in animated conversation about the great issues bursting around us.

Among the twelve were Graham Claytor, my friend from the *Harvard Law Review* and later president of the Southern Railroad and of Amtrak; Bill Cary, chief of the Securities and Exchange Commission in the Kennedy administration; Adrian Fisher of Kennedy's Arms Control and Disarmament Agency; John Oakes of the *New York Times*; Hedley Donovan of *Time-Life*; and a giant roly-poly man from Kentucky named Ed Prichard. Prich, with whom I roomed, roamed the Washington agencies as a supercoordinator, electrifying everyone with his conversational thrusts and parries and even entertaining FDR at the White House with matchless impersonations of FDR's opponents.

After the war, when we went back to our homes, we expected that Prich, then back in Kentucky, would soon be returning to Washington as senator, president, whatever. But it was not to be: in an irresponsible prank in the 1948 elections he was found to have stuffed a ballot box—for what purpose heaven knows. He was convicted and served his time in federal prison. He returned to Lexington, broken, broke, and with a family to support. But for the next thirty years he held to the narrow path of honor, and when he died in 1984 he was enshrined as the father of Kentucky's educational reform.

WORLD WAR II

In January 1943 I reported for military service at the Milwaukee induction center on Edison Street. My draft number had been slow in coming up, but I thought it was about time, for by now World War II was in full swing. At the induction center I was victimized by an old army game I should have been warned against. The sergeant told us ragged recruits: "I want a man with an advanced degree, who speaks a foreign language fluently and has leadership potential." I proudly stepped forward. "Okay, soldier, here's a mop. Go clean up the latrine."

An unheated train bore us to Camp Joseph T. Robinson, near Little Rock, Arkansas. Here I endured the thirteen weeks of basic training, the common fate of about ten million other young Americans. At thirty I was no spring chicken, but I managed to hold my own. I particularly remember one bayonet drill. The instructor demanded that we yell out ferociously at the end of our exercise, to signal that our enemy had been adequately dis-emboweled. Through clumsiness I hit my big toe with my rifle butt just at this moment and let out a yell that could be heard a block away. "That's the way to sound off!" shouted the instructor. It was well-deserved praise.

Like other GIs, I soon learned the army lingo. The army branch in which I served became the "impantry," as opposed to the "calvary." The leather case for a pistol became the "hollister." The globe that fastened a mortar to its base became the "spiritual projection." I felt that I could talk the talk.

An old sweetheart of mine lived in Little Rock—Josephine Heiskell of the family that published the renowned *Arkansas Gazette*. I looked her up, and she and her family were marvelously hospitable to me and to my fellow recruit Klaus Mann, son of the novelist Thomas. So was Ina Harris, mother of my friend Tom Harris of OPA days, who treated me like a son—or better.

Because of these delightful hostesses, and an occasional good book at the camp library, I was generally unavailable for the Saturday night for-ays into Little Rock by my trainee buddies. But I can tell you that, based on their testimony, Little Rock was a veritable Gomorrah. Of course, they may have exaggerated.

Toward the end of my stay at Camp Robinson the word went around that a visit from the commander-in-chief was expected and that the band should be ready to play "Hail to the Chief." I was among those selected for the honor guard and polished my boots to a high luster. I presented arms smartly when the chief passed, jauntily smoking his cigarette. That was as close as I ever got to FDR.

Presently, I was selected to attend the infantry officers' candidate school at Fort Benning, Columbus, Georgia. The battles in North Africa had taken a toll on infantry lieutenants, and more were needed. My class at Benning was the first to be integrated. Along with a collection of young white candidates from the University of Arkansas was a contingent of young black candidates from around the country. Everyone was so busy learning how to command a platoon that no one had time for any racial nonsense.

The infantry school was a rigorous place, every bit as competitive as Harvard Law had been. In July 1948 I got news of the birth of our son, Christopher. In November I won my second lieutenant's bars. Years later, speaking in Columbus, Georgia, at a fund-raising dinner for a colleague, I was pleased to learn that I was enrolled in the Infantry Hall of Fame at Fort Benning.

General officers of the various divisions of the army would gather at each Benning graduation to pick their aides-de-camp. The commanding general of the Seventh Armored Division interviewed me and briefly made me his aide-de-camp. But the general shortly decided he needed a better situation-map draftsman than I was and picked someone else. Maybe it was providential. The Seventh Armored took the important rail center of Metz, France, in September 1944 but executed a "retrograde movement to the rear"—in plain language, a retreat—when the Germans counterattacked. Thus a chance to shorten the war was lost, and the general, and presumably his aide, were in trouble.

I was assigned to the Sixty-third Infantry Division, in training at Camp Van Dorn, Mississippi, during the cold and muddy winter of 1943–1944 and took over as platoon leader of a heavy-machine-gun platoon. There I soon received a lesson in military personnel practices. Morale in my platoon had been low because none of my recruits had even seen a machine gun before. Suddenly, we got a new recruit from Cicero, Illinois, who knew and loved machine guns from his civilian job working for the celebrated mobster Al Capone. Morale in the platoon picked up immediately. But a relapse set in two weeks later when the army decided to send my boy to cooks' and bakers' school, and he was seen no more.

In early spring 1944 I was transferred again, this time to the International Division at the Pentagon in Washington. In early June the International Division, largely concerned with helping the U.S. Army of liberation live off the country as it moved forward into Europe, sent me to join General Eisenhower's Supreme Headquarters Allied Expeditionary Force (SHAEF) at Bushy Park near London.

I arrived on D day. The Nazi buzz bombs, unmanned airplanes armed with heavy warheads, had just started landing in southern England. They were pulverizing homes and pubs and factories all around my billet. We slept in a badly ventilated shelter in Teddington-on-Thames, along with the civilians of the neighborhood. I noticed the effect on ordinary people of this sudden quickening of violent war on the home front. The English had shown magnificent courage during the Battle of Britain three years earlier, going about their business with good cheer all during the Luftwaffe's nightly bombings. But then the Royal Air Force miraculously won the Battle of Britain — "never have so many owed so much to so few" — and people relaxed. To have the terror in the air now suddenly renewed was simply too much; men and women were numbed by it.

My SHAEF duties involved writing military manuals to govern procurement by our advancing armies on the Continent. The manuals, of course, had to be bilingual — English and American. This required the frequent use of slashed phrases — lumber/timber, gasoline/petrol, and panties/knickers come to mind. Commander Eisenhower stood for no nonsense that might turn Brit and Yank against one another in his combined headquarters. You could call an opposite number a son-of-a-bitch, but never, on pain of court-martial, a *British* son-of-a-bitch. I took on a bit of the color of my British colleagues by acquiring a fine pair of high-cut Lotus waterproof boots and a leather jerkin right out of Robin Hood and Sherwood Forest.

During my six weeks at Bushy Park I made many friends among the British officers and "other ranks." I met kilted Highlanders like Peter Eastman, chief of the Maclaren clan, and H. J. Scrimgeor Wedderburn, former secretary of state for Scotland. Among the "other ranks," I especially remember Jack Caesar, bright as hell but doomed to noncommissioned rank because of his definitely non-U accent. I rather suspect that Jack, if he survived, voted against the Tories in the 1945 general election.

I gained much broader exposure to the British character through my new American friend, Sam Katz of Tennessee. Sam was a lifelong Anglophile who had arrived in Britain with the first wave of Yanks. He had used his leave time for a year to cultivate every British bookseller, don, and antiquarian within reach. He kindly brought me along on his intellectual excursions, usually involving some tweedy philosopher reflectively tapping his pipe on the club hearth as he discoursed on the meaning of life. Sam's and my paths crossed again when I came to Congress in 1955. He had become the renowned chief of the Federal Reserve's foreign economic division, and I enjoyed testing my heretical views on international money against his firmly held official views.

Operation Overlord, meanwhile, had secured its beachhead and closed the Falaise Gap, trapping many Wehrmacht divisions and marking the beginning of its long retreat to Germany's borders. In mid-July our group established itself at Granville in Normandy. At the liberation of Paris in August 1944 I was assigned to the newly set-up SHAEF mission to France.

I'll never forget riding in my jeep the last twenty miles from Fontainebleau to Paris, through huge crowds of welcoming French holding signs that read "Hommage à Nos Liberateurs." The welcomers included lots of adorable French maidens, got up delightfully in chemically dubious wartime French cosmetics; their kisses may have been responsible for the dermatitis suffered by my GI jeep driver.

We arrived at our temporary billets at the Hotel Meurice on the Rue de Rivoli the morning after the Oberkommando Wehrmacht moved out. With a princely flourish the Meurice head waiter lifted the silver bell from our first dinner: SPAM!

Liberation day was the day the French, humiliated and divided, came together. Even the *flics,* Paris's not always admired police, conducted themselves with great gallantry in mopping up the pockets of German resistance and briefly found themselves heroes.

I stayed with the SHAEF mission through Armistice Day. November 11, 1944, saw a grand parade down the Champs Elysées. Combat troops from our three nations, and Churchill with his cigar and de Gaulle, an elegant dinosaur in his command car, streamed by. De Gaulle, the spirit of the liberation to the French people, had with his imperial manner infuriated the British Foreign Office and our State Department. They denied him recognition as the government of France and conducted relationships through a group of French technocrats with no visible popular support. On the eve of my transfer to SHAEF headquarters in Versailles, I wrote my last memorandum for the mission to France, through channels I hoped would reach as far up as possible. In essence, my message was: "Look, we're in a war: the longer we humiliate de Gaulle by denying him recognition, the longer he'll bear a grudge against us." His grudge, it turned out, lasted the rest of his life.

My next post, during the winter of 1944–1945, was back at SHAEF, now headquartered in Louis XIV's royal stables out at Versailles. I have two memories. One is of the admirable Huchon family in whose modest cottage I was billeted. Both were schoolteachers, always likely to be bastions of French republicanism. When I left for the front, Papa Huchon, abed suffering from malnutrition, paid me his highest compliment by calling me a *chic type.* Their daughter Jeanette came to America years later, and I caught up with her when she taught at Penn State.

The second memory has to do with the setting up of the first free newspaper on German soil. Aachen, home of the great Charlemagne, had just fallen to Allied forces in October 1944. I was sent out to get a newspaper started. We found presses, newsprint, reporters, and a publisher who answered every command with *Jawohl*. In a matter of days we set the *Aachener Nachrichtung* afloat.

Meanwhile, I had been lobbying to get transferred to a division. This necessitated my finding a substitute for my job at SHAEF. He turned out to be my old friend from Washington days, Charles Owsley, who had been languishing with the Eighth Air Force at High Wycombe near Oxford.

So in early March 1945 I was conveyed by jeep to the Seventy-fifth Infantry Division as it lay on the left bank of the Rhine near Duisburg, Germany, waiting for the Rhine crossing. The Seventy-fifth had recently arrived in the European theater and had just won its spurs in the Battle of the Bulge. Its shoulder patch—red, white, and blue with a 75—frequently made the French mistake us for one of their own—the French 75.

I had descended from SHAEF, at the top of the command structure, through army group, army corps, to division. Below us were regiment, battalion, company, platoon, and finally squad—the basic twelve-man team of the infantry division. My duty, as a captain, was that of assistant G-3, military operations. G-1 was personnel, G-2 intelligence, and G-4 supply. The G-3 commander, my boss, was Col. Robert Dean, a professor of architecture at the Massachusetts Institute of Technology before the war. We wrote the orders, supervised how they were being carried out, and coordinated the activities of the various nonintegral units attached to us.

At least two of these units were very dear to us. One was the army air force's close-support planes. When our infantry was pinned down by hostile fire from a bunker or other fortification, we could call on one of these pilots to dive in with machine gun or cannon to interdict whatever was holding us up.

Another good buddy was a Scottish tank battalion, Lothian and Border Yeomanry, the equivalent of one of our national guard outfits. Its tanks had flame throwers ("crocodiles") for use against enemy bunkers and front-mounted rotating chains ("flails") to detonate enemy mine fields. These gallant lowland Scots opened many a tough spot for us, and almost all were killed doing their duty. These close-support tank battalions were, in my view, much more effective than some of our highly touted armored divisions, which spectacularly swept a hundred miles a day but behind enemy lines where little could stop them.

A third attachment unit was our antiaircraft, about whose effectiveness I am still unsure. This unit reported downing a significant number of German Messerschmidts, but higher echelon later reported that the total coincided ominously with the losses suffered on the same front by British Spitfires. This puts me in mind of a retired admiral who in 1941 had been a spirited dancer at the Sulgrave Club balls in Washington. He had the distinction of having skippered the first U.S. destroyer to sink a British warship in the English Channel in World War I.

With our orders for the Rhine crossing due any day, we were concerned that the Germans dug in on the other side were somehow infiltrating our lines and scouting our formations. In fact, a number of infiltrators had been captured, and they confessed that they had crossed the Rhine in their rubber foldboats and simply landed unapprehended on our shore. Something was wrong here: our maps showed every jetty jutting out on our side, and our defensive patrols were covering every inch of ground between the jetties. I was sent down that night to find out what could be the matter. After crawling along the Rhine flood plain for several hours, I did find out. There was one more jetty than our maps showed, so that the two patrols were leaving a gap of several hundred yards, which the Germans were using for infiltrating at will. We fixed up our patrols and suffered no more infiltration.

Now came the order for the crossing. The crossing was to be accomplished by a parachute drop on the far side, then a pontoon bridge, then a more permanent steel structure known as a Bailey bridge. The crossing was to be preceded by the heaviest artillery bombardment in history. My job was to hole up on the top onion of a baroque church to transmit the message if the assault had to be canceled. But the Seventy-fifth maintained its beachhead, made an assault crossing of the Ruhr Canal, and accepted the surrender of Dortmund. Soon our forward task force made contact with a task force from our armies to the south, and the Ruhr Pocket was sealed off in early April 1945. Our POW pens were bulging with about 325,000 prisoners. Gen. George Marshall called it the largest double envelopment in American military history. The end was now in sight.

The Seventy-fifth was directed to occupy that part of Westphalia that lies between Paderborn on the east, Lüdenscheid on the south, Wuppertal on the west, and Dortmund on the north. Now *we* were the occupiers. No German death camps were in our zone, but we uncovered several slave labor camps that were brutal enough, with their Russian and Slavic prisoners near starvation. Even so, these persecuted slave laborers gave their best space, and a bouquet of pussy willow, to their goddess, the slave camp ballerina. We also uncovered the salt mine in which Hermann Göring had stashed some of the art treasures looted from the rest of Europe. I recall a beautiful Van Gogh landscape that had developed deep strands of spinach from its long sojourn in the mine. We gently removed the fungus, but it returned every night until we carefully packed the masterpiece and sent it on up to higher echelons and safety.

Nor did we overlook recreational facilities. Included in our zone was a large reservoir lake, still intact despite our repeated attempts to bomb the retaining dam. On that lake we found a beautiful mahogany speedboat in mint condition. We quickly liberated it, rechristened it the *Alice Kaput,* and used her joyously for R&R.

The defeated Germans were not entirely hospitable. One stunt was to stretch an almost invisible razor wire across the roads our vehicles had to pass, presaging certain beheading. Fortunately, our motor maintenance unit immediately adopted a preventative—a vertical steel bar attached to the bumper of every jeep. This did prevent decapitation, though at the price of being snapped violently backward.

I encountered a less gruesome problem while negotiating with a saucy young German woman, who had fled the bombed city for the countryside, to do my laundry. Unfortunately for my dignity, the *Wäscherei* negotiation took place in a cellar with an extremely low ceiling, on which I kept painfully bumping my steel helmet. The defeated German laundress had the temerity to laugh at the conquering American.

We heard sorrowfully of FDR's death and joyfully of the armistice and the fall of Hitler. The Seventy-fifth's commanding general immediately ordered me to write and produce a history of the division. I accomplished this task speedily, in the most pedestrian prose: "Baker Company of 1st Battalion, 289th Infantry Regiment jumped off at 0:400 hours, etc." But the paper on which to print it was nowhere to be found. I requisitioned a large army truck and scoured central Germany until I finally stumbled on the former map center of the Wehrmacht near Wiesbaden. It was full of beautiful glossy paper never used for its intended purpose of invasion maps of England. Quickly commandeered, my spoils of war allowed the "history" to be produced within weeks of the war's end.

Over the years I kept up with the old Seventy-fifth. Once I spoke at its convention—didn't recognize a soul. The outfit's infantry commander, Brig. Gen. Gerald St. Claire Mickle, sent me a Christmas card every year, with the Stars and Stripes flying proudly over his Alabama home.

MILITARY GOVERNMENT

The war in Europe was now over, but I was still many months shy of sufficient points to qualify me for a discharge and home. The future of the Seventy-fifth Division, now redeploying to Reims in France, looked unexciting. The action, I thought, might now be in the new military government about to be set up in the U.S. zone of occupation in southwest Germany. So I hitched a ride to Paris and burst in upon Gen. William Draper, the brilliant Wall Street investment banker who was heading up the planning for military government. Price control would be one of its major functions, and I explained my OPA experience. Draper offered me the job of heading control in the U.S. sector, a general's slot on the organizational chart but one a captain was very pleased to accept.

So began the last six months of my European service. Our headquarters was the enormous and unharmed I. G. Farben office building in Frankfurt. Friendly General Eisenhower again held sway, always displaying that empathy for the lower ranks that was the secret of his military, and later his political, popularity. When some officious major guarding Hitler's mountain lair at Berchtesgaden required visiting GIs to climb up on foot to the "eagle's nest" and posted a placard restricting admission on the elevator to "Field Grade Officers Only"—majors and up—Ike had the placard unceremoniously tossed over the mountainside.

Finding "good Germans" in Hitler's devastated Reich became one of the most extensive affirmative action programs in history. They were not easy to find. Two who resoundingly passed the test were brought to my attention in a letter from my old friend Sophie Schroeder, administrator of the Milwaukee Children's Hospital in which my family had long been interested. As a young nurse in the 1920s, Sophie had emigrated from Germany and had risen to the top of Children's Hospital by her intelligence and charm. She wrote that she had two elderly aunts living in a village near Frankfurt who were having a hard time, and she asked whether I could get some nourishment for them. So, armed with a couple of CARE packages, I found them in the little village and heard their story. They were Quakers, a tiny sect in Hitler's Germany, and had set up their home as a station on the underground railroad to shelter Jewish émigrés on their way to Switzerland. Dear souls, they seemed not to know what awaited them had they been caught or that they had done anything extraordinary. They were grateful for the CARE packages.

Gen. Lucius Clay, a proconsul worthy of the Republic, was in charge of the military government. Early on he called me to his office: "Captain, the displaced persons down at Stuttgart are conducting a black market in the central square, and it's a disgrace. I want you to go down there and break it up!" "Yes sir!" I replied, and took off immediately for Stuttgart. The square did indeed look like a medieval Nizhni Novgorod, with a thousand homeless Slavic refugees bartering cigarettes and cameras for whatever they could get. I arranged for the military police to clear a bombed-out area a few blocks away and to invite the black marketeers to transfer their activities there. I was able to report back to General Clay that my mission had been accomplished.

Many of my former colleagues from the OPA staff were converging on Germany. With Dave Ginsburg, Carl Auerbach, Tom Harris, Taylor Ostrander, and others we set up what amounted to an OPA-am-Rhine. It soon became apparent that price controls, which we were maintaining in their original Nazi form, were not working and could not work. In its final days the Third Reich had turned on the printing press and flooded the country with paper marks much too numerous for the trickle of goods being produced. What was needed, I became convinced, was currency reform in which all would have to turn in their bundle of inflated marks for a few solid new marks, after which price controls could be progressively removed as the market responded with newly produced goods.

My conclusion was strongly supported by Dr. Franz Eucken, an anti-Hitler economist who miraculously had survived. In our search for capable and untainted Germans to operate the provisional government we were setting up, we had found him among the ruins of the University of Freiburg. He must be credited with much of the sensible economics that helped the new Germany rise from the ashes.

But my lobbying efforts for currency reform were unsuccessful. Price control was embedded in the military government plan and had to remain there until the plan was changed. Almost my last act before departing for the United States at the end of 1945 was to send up through channels one of my more audacious memoranda, couched in the regulation format of "completed staff work." It advocated that the military either ordain an immediate currency reform, followed by price decontrol, or acknowledge publicly that, because currency reform was impossible and price controls useless, price controls were to be suspended immediately. I hoped that this would spur fast action. Sadly, currency reform was delayed until 1948, when it was finally put into effect and became the foundation of the generation-long German "economic miracle."

In midsummer 1945 we heard of the bomb over Hiroshima and of Japan's capitulation. Overwhelmed with joy at the war's end, how could I do other than cheer President Truman's decision to drop the bomb? Today the world needs an equally gutsy presidential decision to ask all the nuclear powers to join us in steadily eliminating their nuclear arsenals.

In January 1946 I finally received orders to proceed home, together with a promotion to major. At Antwerp I boarded a Liberty ship bound for Sandy Hook, New Jersey. I was the ship's ranking officer and commander. The only other officer, besides the civilian crew, was Lt. Maurice Wolkomir from Milwaukee, whom I had known as the federal probation officer for Wisconsin. Morrie, though badly down with yellow fever, kept gamely playing his liberated near-Stradivarius violin during the long voyage. It took us twenty-one days to sail from Antwerp to New York. With our plates buckling in the January gales, we barely made it.

The ship's complement of enlisted men, seven hundred strong, were all from segregated black construction battalions and all as eager to get home as we were. As commanding officer, I observed a remarkable example of market capitalism in action. Each of the seven hundred had come aboard loaded with the spoils of the Continent—daggers, cameras, minor objects of art. A crap game developed in the latrine as we slipped down the Schelde to the North Sea. It lasted three days, at the end of which all the loot had passed into the hands of the three foremost crapshooters.

It was my duty to give "Information and Education" talks to the troops. The current tutorial was about the recent staggering news of nuclear fission, and I prepared my talk to get my audience's attention over the pitching and rolling of our Liberty ship. "Do you men realize that one piece of uranium the size of your little finger has as much energy as all the coal in the world?" "Man, that's a lot of energy!" "And do you realize that if we harness this energy for the public good, mankind hereafter will have to work only an hour or two a day?" I got a standing ovation, but I've worried over the last half-century whether I'd ever run into one of my oversold and possibly angry listeners.

We finally made New York harbor. My troops were demobilized, Lieutenant Wolkomir installed in a military hospital, and I on my way to Fort Sheridan on the North Shore of Chicago. Discharged late one wintry night, I taxied straight to my wife's family home in Winnetka. She and our little son, Chris, now three, had been spending the war years there while she completed her master's degree in economics at the University of Chicago. This was a happy night all around.

My three years in the military was another important milestone on my way toward becoming a cog in our democracy. The democratic life requires that you know, and perhaps even love, all sorts of people. For this the army provided almost ideal adverse conditions.

3

The Rocky Road
to Capitol Hill
(1946–1955)

THE 1948 MAYORALTY

My return to Milwaukee from Washington and Europe in January 1946 was, in a way, a replay of my return from Ithaca and Cambridge in 1936. I went back to the law firm of Quarles Spence and Quarles, this time as a junior partner. I joyfully introduced my spouse and family to my old friends and their spouses and families.

But the differences between 1936 and 1946 were great. Now I was married, with a wife I adored and a family that was growing. We installed ourselves in one of the nineteenth-century brick three-story row houses near downtown known as Ogden Row, for which I paid my life savings of $4,500. Our second son, Michael, was born that October, a harbinger of the postwar baby boom. When Margaret went into labor, she and I were chasing butterflies in western Wisconsin, and we barely made it to the maternity ward at Milwaukee Hospital in time.

We loved our neighbors in the Row, among them Bill Norris, the veteran *Milwaukee Sentinel* reporter; Stevie Miller, a pal of our kids' and later an international rock star; Phil Robinson, public-spirited Northwestern Mutual Life executive; Karl Brocken, industrial designer; Don Smith, inventor and industrialist; and Hannah Mortensen, supercook.

I had decided that a public life, at least modestly on the left, was what I wanted. Casting around for a veterans' organization to join, I picked the newly created American Veterans Committee (AVC). With its motto of "Citizens First, Veterans Second," the AVC infuriated the traditional veterans' groups such as the American Legion and the Veterans of Foreign Wars, which viewed things the other way around. The AVC was spearheaded by such national leaders as Richard Bolling of Missouri, later a Democratic member of Congress from Missouri; Gilbert Harrison and Michael Straight, later publishers of the *New Republic;* and Charles Bolte, a splendid orator. All took the liberal position on the current critical issues—civil rights and liberties, housing, full employment.

On foreign policy, however, its leaders saw the iron curtain clanking down. They determined to keep AVC and the country from falling into the Soviet embrace. This involved a pitched battle at the 1946 AVC convention, its first. It was held in Milwaukee, and I was the welcoming local chairman. Behind the scenes, a slate of candidates backed by the Communist Party/USA almost staged a coup but was stopped without dragging the conflict to center stage.

Depression and war had brought about a serious shortage of decent affordable housing throughout the country, and Milwaukee was as troubled as anywhere. Veterans particularly could not find even a garret to rent. I determined to do something about it. The Wisconsin legislature during the war, under the leadership of Democratic state senator Robert Tehan, had passed the Urban Renewal Act. The act offered tax benefits to non-profit organizations that proposed to tear down "substandard" housing and build modern low-rent apartments in their place. I put together a coalition of Clem Kalvelage, a respected real estate man; Peter Schoeman, dean of the building trades unions; and Mike Meyer, an architect and friend. We formed the Milwaukee Urban Redevelopment Corporation and proposed to demolish a block of substandard houses in the Red Arrow Park area between the Milwaukee Public Library and Marquette University and replace them with a high-rise low-rent apartment building. Under the law we needed a two-thirds vote of the Milwaukee Common Council before we could proceed. Our plan drew quick public support, but unforeseen difficulties soon developed. John Koerner, the longtime alderman for the area, lived in one of the houses slated for demolition and led the charge against the project. Worse, Tehan also lived in the demolition area, having moderately restored *his* "substandard" home. He was kind enough not to fight the project, but he did not support it, either.

When the vote came up in the common council, we got 14 votes to 13 for our opponents, many fewer than we needed for a two-thirds victory. Looking back, a project that required demolishing one person's home in order to house another was not very fair. My only excuse is that it was the only mechanism available and that I was extremely ignorant.

All this activity was making me better known around town. Thus, when sitting mayor John Bohn, a pleasant old man who disliked ruffling anyone's feathers, announced that he would not run again in the April 1948 mayoralty election, I soon announced my candidacy. So did twenty other candidates, among them longtime former mayor Dan Hoan, now grown old and irascible; Art Ehrman, darling of the politically powerful Fraternal Order of Eagles; Henry Maier, another young veteran; handsome John Fleming; Ruth Froemming, a former Ziegfeld Follies star; and Frank Zeidler, brother of the boy wonder Carl Zeidler, who had toppled Dan Hoan in 1940 but met an untimely death at sea in 1943.

I campaigned as an activist candidate, with detailed plans on what I proposed to do about jobs, homes, taxes. I remained nonpartisan, because I had support from a broad cross-section of the electorate. My backers included conservatives, like banker William Brumder and veterans' leader Tracy Hale, and progressives, like labor leader Jake Friedrick and school board member George Hampel.

My most devoted supporter, albeit behind the scenes, was veteran *Milwaukee Journal* reporter and drama and music critic Richard M. Davis. Dick, though the son of a Methodist minister, would never refuse a chilled martini nor a fast game of pool. But he had an enormous heart. Early on he wrote impassioned pieces in the *Journal* about Milwaukee's impoverished African American citizens huddled in their North Side ghettos. A little book of Davis's articles was published after his death. For its muscular writing it ought to be in every reporter's library. Dick took a shine to me early, urged me to run, and on the quiet wrote a number of my speeches (he had no role in the paper's political coverage).

In the primary I came in second, moderately behind Frank Zeidler. Frank had the benefit of a well-known name, inherited from his brother, Carl; a good record on the school board; and a sizable cadre of old socialists who admired his loyalty and integrity. Frank's "socialism," as he practiced it in his twelve years in the mayor's office, ran toward honest government with a modest bent toward helping the underdog. In short, he deserved to win, and win he did, by the same margin as in the primary.

(Twelve years later, when Mayor Zeidler retired in 1960, I impulsively decided to run for mayor a second time. My principal opponent, state Sen. Henry Maier, outcampaigned me and won. Some political pundits have attributed my defeat to the famous "sleeping bag incident." During the mayor's race I was living in my late mother's home on Maryland and Newberry on Milwaukee's East Side. Because the house was undergoing an extensive renovation, I lived in an attic room. And because the weather was cold, I slept in a sleeping bag. This critical fact was duly reported in the *Milwaukee Journal* and endlessly repeated. To this day I stubbornly cannot see what the sleeping bag had to do with the election; I am told that it sounded vaguely libidinous and disqualifying. At any rate, I lost. Considering that I was easily reelected to Congress for the next quarter century, I have comfortably concluded that the voters simply wanted me to represent them on Capitol Hill rather than in City Hall.)

When Dick Davis called me from the newspaper after the returns began to come in on election night—"It doesn't look good"—he seemed to be taking my defeat more seriously than I did. But rejection did slowly sink in. My law practice was nearly in ruins. That summer the Madison group of youthful veterans starting to rebuild the moribund Wisconsin Democratic Party asked whether I would join their ticket for the November 1948 state elections—Carl Thompson for governor, me for lieutenant governor, Tom Fairchild for attorney general. Tentatively, I agreed. But the next day I stopped in at the Milwaukee County Democratic Party headquarters, headed by Charley Greene, the old-line state chairman and patronage dispenser. Because he was the titular head of the party, I wanted to know his thoughts on my proposed candidacy. His thoughts were choleric— why would I want to do a thing like this—a conspiracy obviously directed against his organization? He would see to it that I had plenty of opposition in the primary. Mine was hardly a profile in courage, but the next day I called my Madison colleagues to say that I had changed my mind, felt I couldn't undertake an intraparty fight in my own backyard so soon after my mayoralty defeat, and would they please find another candidate for lieutenant governor. My confusion produced plenty of bad feeling among the Madisonians. This falling out, part of the larger Madison-Milwaukee sniping of those days, went on for some time.

THE MARSHALL PLAN

I was not to be at loose ends for long. As 1948 progressed, the Marshall Plan was emerging from Congress. It was a happy amalgam of softhearted compassion for the people of a devastated Europe and a hardheaded effort to save them from turning in despair to Soviet-led communism. It appealed deeply to my instinct that America must resist a relapse into the isolationism that had so scarred us in the interval between the two world wars.

Paul Hoffman had just been appointed chief of the fledgling Economic Cooperation Administration (ECA), which was independent of the State Department and ran the Marshall Plan, when he came to Milwaukee for a speech in the fall of 1948. We talked about my joining the legal staff of the ECA in Paris. In November 1948 I signed on for the new job, subject to the loyalty check of the day. Though I passed the test without challenge, the comments of some of those interviewed tell a lot about the mind-set of respectable Milwaukee in the 1940s.[1]

By Thanksgiving Day Margaret, our two young sons, and I were aboard a plane approaching Paris, where for the next fourteen months I was to be assistant, then deputy, then acting general counsel under Ambassador Milton Katz. As we came in for a landing at Le Bourget, our younger son,

Mike, was roaming the aisle and bloodied his nose when the bumpy flight caused him to hit the overhead rack. The welcoming ambassador diplomatically declined to take note of the gore.

The legal office of ECA/Europe was a young lawyer's dream. There were four of us—Milt Katz, later for many years the head of Harvard Law School's international legal studies; Kingman Brewster, who became president of Yale; Roger Fisher, professor at Harvard Law School and inventor of the negotiating process known as "getting to yes"; and me. Our little law firm believed that we were engaged in a great enterprise, that rather than live a life apart we should mingle with the Marshall Plan's administrators and economists, and that our legal pronouncements should be written in a language that was easy to understand and a pleasure to read.

Above all, we believed with the Marshall Plan's leaders that our role was not to direct the Europeans but to help them to help themselves. We worked closely with the sixteen countries that made up the Marshall Plan's governing body, the Committee for European Economic Cooperation. From this CEEC grew the present flourishing OECD, Organization for Economic Cooperation and Development.

I can remember helping draft the European Payments Agreement, which opened up trade between what had been fiercely protectionist nations. I consulted in Frankfurt with the drafters of the Basic Law for the new Federal Republic of Germany and went to Dublin to aid our mission to Ireland in reopening mines that had not been worked since the days of the Caesars. Back in Washington, I helped deputy administrator Bill Foster construct a program for visits by European workers to study American productivity. These were exciting times and exciting tasks.

Our Paris office in the Hotel Talleyrand on the Place de la Concorde was a model of bureaucratic democracy. We of the lesser ranks were encouraged to speak our minds. In fact, some of us—who were used to grabbing a croque monsieur for lunch at the snack bar—formed our informal Snack Bar Policy Board—economist Taylor Ostrander, labor specialist Sol Ozer, journalist Waldemar Nielson, and administrator Everett Bellows among them. Together we pondered long over many a great question—how to get the Common Market and the European Community started; how to encourage labor unions that would be neither communist nor limp; how to ensure that three Franco-Prussian wars in a century were enough.

One reason Marshall planners were a happy breed was that we admired our bosses. They were supposed to be Democrats and Republicans in equal proportions, but it was hard to tell by their actions which was which. As in the brave days of old,

> Then none was for the party,
> And all were for the state.

Get on with the job was our leaders' leitmotif. They were Republicans like Paul Hoffman, who made sturdy Studebakers and was soon to make a sturdy Atlantic Community, and Bill Foster, who looked as if he had been sent by Central Casting to play the clean-cut American executive and conducted himself accordingly, and Democrats like the Bruces, of the old Maryland-Virginia Tidewater aristocracy, with their sense of civic duty, and Averell Harriman, determined to excel at everything from international diplomacy to lawn croquet. What an inspiration they all were, and how we need them now.

What was the Marshall Plan's accomplishment, from the vantage point of fifty years? Rather than drown in statistics, let us look at the life of the people of the tiny village in southwest France where Margaret and I have been spending our summers since our retirement. Back in the forties, the women did the family laundry by beating it against the rocks at the river's edge. Drinking water had to be carried by hand up the steep bluff. Glad that the war was over, men worked long and hard for a meager living. There were no telephones, nor electricity for that matter.

Today all is prosperity in the little village. World War II is almost forgotten, and a German family recently moved into the village without incident. Running water permits washing machines. All have telephones, often equipped with cute little Minitel computers that make life easy. Some already have high-definition television. All enjoy health care and services from day care to elder care as a matter of right. The Marshall Plan brought sensational growth rates to postwar France, and a fair share trickled down to our little village.

The Marshall Plan was not carried out in order to wring gratitude from its recipients. But to a surprising extent it has done just that. The Germans have concocted the German Marshall Fund, which brings to America all sorts of examples of contemporary European culture, from city planning to early education. The British have founded the Marshall Scholarships to give young Americans a touch of the British university. I was delighted to go to Vienna a few years ago as the guest of Chancellor Bruno Kreisky to dedicate an Austrian memorial to the Marshall Plan in front of the historic St. Stephen's cathedral.

Could the Marshall Plan, aimed at the reconstruction of war-devastated Europe, be a model for other worthy activities? Hardly a month goes by without someone's suggesting a Marshall Plan for impoverished Appalachia, for our stricken cities, for troubled Africa. Usually, the focus is on the $13 billion check the United States wrote as the material component of European recovery.

But the Marshall Plan was about much more than money. Rather, its genius lay in its emphasis on cooperative planning and action by the plan's beneficiaries. The countries had to agree on how to divide the money and how it was to be spent. The habit of working together engendered by the plan was shortly put to even more important use in the building of the European Community.

This liberating core of the Marshall Plan—the need for cooperation—deserves to be invoked more frequently. At home our federal system is creaking, and state and local governments are having difficulty carrying out their responsibilities in metropolitan areas and in central-city ghettos. I believe that although government should be as close to the people as possible, the federal government is the one best able to administer an equalizing revenue system of progressive income and estate taxes. Why not provide unrestricted federal fiscal aid to states and localities, provided only that the states, on a regional basis, work out plans to modernize state and local governments? I introduced legislation to that effect back in the 1970s; it was favorably reported out of committee but sank without trace when the special interests of existing governments combined against it.

Abroad lie equally promising opportunities for the Marshall Plan's spirit. Confronted with the aftermath of the cold war, Secretary of State Madeline Albright, in her address at Harvard in June 1997 commemorating the fiftieth anniversary of the Marshall Plan, called for America to "take advantage of the historic opportunity that now exists to bring the world together in an international system based on democracy, open markets, law and a commitment to peace."

John W. Tuthill, former ambassador to Brazil and U.S. delegate to the Organization for Economic Cooperation and Development, and I have been proposing a "Concert of the Democracies," a representative organization for the world's industrialized democracies that would replace at least five of today's duplicating and ineffectual political-economic groupings (see Chapter 4). This looks like just what Secretary Albright was proposing. Unfortunately, the Clinton administration has instead focused on the military alliance NATO rather than on a new political-economic organization like our proposal for a Concert of the Democracies as its chosen means of meeting Albright's goal. Admitting some countries and excluding others from NATO, which was forged in the cold war, is likely to lead to unnecessary friction and to make the Russians feel increasingly downgraded and resentful. What the countries of the collapsed Soviet empire really needed was membership in a political-economic organization whose political goal was humane, law-abiding politics and whose economic goal was free markets with a human face. This was the formula that saved the West in the years after World War II. The best that can be said for enlarging NATO is that it was irrelevant.

Our year in Paris for the Marshall Plan was memorable, not just because of the job but because the City of Light was a magical place in which to live. Gaiety and good food had long since returned, but it was still possible to park on any Paris street. We took weekend jaunts to the beautiful cathedral at Chartres or to the forest of Fontainebleau. There were stars to see and hear—Edith Piaf at the Empire or the eighty-year-old Mistinguette at the Casino. There were traveling Americans to welcome, like the great judge Learned Hand; journalists like Teddy White and Cyrus Sulzberger; my old OPA boss Leon Henderson; Reinhold Niebuhr, the theologian of original sin; and Myrna Loy herself.

We lived in the once-elegant house of the Comtesse de Waziers across the street from Napoleon's Tomb at Les Invalides. The basement kitchen was commodious, but in keeping with the French preference for the start of the alimentary canal rather than the finish, the toilet was in a miserable constricted alcove accessible only from the winding staircase.

In this house my trusting wife fell victim to a classic confidence game. A distinguished-looking visitor appeared one day, produced a large envelope containing a will he had drawn for the Comtesse de Waziers, and asked Margaret to convey it to her when she next called to collect the rent. Ah! there was the little matter of the five-hundred-franc deposit on the will. Not to worry, replied Margaret, as the gentleman's eyes glazed over in gratitude; *she* would make the deposit and recover it from the comtesse. The envelope, of course, turned out to contain nothing but newspaper clips, the comtesse knew of no will, and poor Margaret was soon over at the police station telling her sad tale. The police were radiant: *Encore le grand escroc!*—The great con man has struck again!

In October 1949, at the American Hospital in Paris, our daughter, Jacqueline, was born, named after our old friend of many years, Mme. Jacqueline Lizotte. A few Sundays later Margaret, the two little boys, and I were wheeling the new arrival around the neighborhood in our snazzy perambulator, a regular Hispano-Suiza of chrome and cabriolet irons. As we passed the great dome of Les Invalides, a scraggly fellow came at me from the shadows proferring "dirty postcards" of ladies clad only in high-button shoes. As I recoiled in horror, four of his colleagues dragged him back, shouting, "Respect yourself! This is a fine gentleman on a Sunday outing." Family values still counted in Paris in 1949.

At the end of our year in December 1949 we boarded the rakish French liner *Île de France* at Cherbourg, and little Mike, now four, immediately tried out the shower in our cabin, drenching himself and his pretty sailor suit. It had barely dried before we reached New York.

Back in Milwaukee, we fitted snugly into our old Ogden Row home. Soon after our return, William Macauley, the district attorney, asked me to become special prosecutor, along with respected Republican lawyer Herbert Mount, for the newly impaneled grand jury investigating municipal corruption. During the next months we compiled evidence leading to convictions for what passed in squeaky-clean 1950 Milwaukee for corruption—such as an alderman who had traded favors to an auto dealer for a prized Buick.

DEMOCRATIC ORGANIZING COMMITTEE

Meanwhile, the new Democratic Organizing Committee (DOC)—the culmination of efforts by new Wisconsin Democrats like Carl Thompson, James Doyle, Horace Willkie, Patrick Lucey, John Reynolds, Gaylord Nelson, and me—was close to its goal of taking over the Wisconsin Democratic Party.

The DOC had come into existence because young veterans returning from the war looked at Wisconsin's political parties and decided that they failed to satisfy the need for forward-looking government.

The Progressives had ended their brief life as a third political party two years earlier, on March 17, 1946. Young Bob La Follette, with another Senate election looming, had told the Progressive Party convention in Portage that he would run as a Republican: "The Democratic party of this state is a machine-minded organization without principle or program. I am convinced that we have a better chance to put our Progressive ideals on the law books if we go into the Republican party. Wisconsin has always been a Republican state—and by this I don't mean a reactionary state."

But La Follette was defeated in the September 1946 Republican primary by Joe McCarthy. The GOP now became a solidly conservative party. It obviously was not the place for progressive-minded young veterans. But the Wisconsin Democratic Party was controlled by reactionaries whose main aim in life was to dispense federal patronage—postmasterships, judgeships, jobs for marshals, positions in the U.S. attorney's office, and so on.

In 1948 the founders of the DOC proclaimed their new movement "the only surviving legitimate heir of the Progressive movement founded by Old Bob La Follette. . . . Peace and stability in the world; freedom, equality and security at home: these are our high aims. To achieve these aims, we seek to promote and to preserve liberal democratic government everywhere— abroad, in America, in Wisconsin."

We of the DOC believed that the true foundation of a political party was the neighborhood—Thomas Jefferson's "ward republic." You could visit a Democratic ward unit in those heady days and hear earnest debate in progress—on a national health program, the United Nations, affordable housing, foreign aid, a loophole-free income tax.

The Young Turks of the DOC did have one ally in the old-line Democratic Party—state senator Robert Tehan of Milwaukee. Of liberal outlook, he had written the Urban Redevelopment Act under which I had tried to bring off my Red Arrow housing project in 1947. Tehan advised and encouraged the Young Turks to take over the party and to run for public office themselves. By 1949 the DOC-ers were sufficiently in control of the party machinery to secure for Tehan an appointment as U.S. district judge for Wisconsin's Eastern District from a grateful President Truman.

Judge Tehan continued to be my friend and mentor all his life. His son Bob, Jr., was for many years my congressional home secretary.

Despite its takeover of the Democratic Party, the DOC was still a long way from winning elections. In Madison, Gov. Walter Kohler, Jr., and the GOP held all the state offices and both houses of the legislature. In Washington, Republicans Alexander Wiley and Joseph McCarthy were entrenched in the Senate. In the House, Clem Zablocki of Milwaukee's South Side was the sole Democrat in a ten-person Wisconsin congressional delegation.

ATTORNEY GENERAL'S RACE

Nonetheless, we boldly entered the 1950 race—Carl Thompson for governor again; Tom Fairchild, this time for senator against Wiley; and I for attorney general. I had a worthy and tough opponent in the Democratic primary, Robert Arthur of Madison, who had scored a breakthrough by getting elected Dane County district attorney. I won the nomination in a squeaker and was grateful to Bob Arthur for his generous support in the general election.

My campaign, conducted mainly from my station wagon, which was equipped with a loudspeaker and a "Reuss for Attorney-General" cartop, took me into all seventy-one of Wisconsin's counties. Wisconsin Democratic candidates in those days economized on travel costs by putting up in each other's homes. Pat Lucey, then campaigning for Congress in southwestern Wisconsin, was my host at his parents' ancestral home, reminiscent of Mark Twain days, at Ferryville on the Mississippi.

At Green Bay I stayed with John Reynolds, also running for Congress, and his young family. Early one morning, on my way out to a plant gate, I was stopped by the milkman: "Mr. Reynolds, can you pay something on your milk bill?" Trying to resolve the problem for my friend, I muttered that happy days would soon be here again and cheerily told him not to worry. I was later told that the bill was promptly paid. Reynolds and Lucey both went on to become first-rate governors of Wisconsin in later decades. Our last child, Anne, was born amid all this electioneering.

Whenever I could, I combined my 1950 campaigning with trout fishing. I always carried a rod and net in my car and between engagements fished many of Wisconsin's famous trout streams. Pinky Rice, in the weekly newspaper of Sparta, reported that "Democratic attorney-general candidate Henry Reuss fished the La Crosse River downstream from the iron bridge at Angelo Tuesday night, later speaking at a rally on courthouse square." Once I was addressing a multitude of about six from the bandstand in Lodi right next to Lodi Creek. A wading angler latched onto a fish and shouted, "Anybody got a net?" I interrupted my speech, got my net from the car, handed it over, watched him land a nice ten-inch brook trout, and returned to my speech.

But the 1950 campaign was not all speckled trout. My Republican opponent, Vernon Thomson of Richland Center (later governor and a member of Congress), was a tough guy, and he sensed my vulnerability. "The socialite socialist," he called me, adding, "He was born with a silver foot in his mouth!"—thirty years before Texas governor Anne Richards, speaking of George Bush, stole the line.

What really sealed the fate of all us Democrats in 1950 was the Korean War. I supported "Harry Truman's war," which was fought under the banner of the United Nations against a North Korean invasion. But the people of Wisconsin emphatically did not support it. Instead, they blamed targets closer to home, like Truman and Secretary of State Dean Acheson, for committing U.S. troops to the conflict. Being a Democrat was an especially hazardous occupation. One Saturday morning I had my loudspeaker going strong at the farmers' market in Wausau. "Are you a Republican or a Democrat?" inquired a dear old lady who closely resembled Whistler's mother. "I'm a Democrat, ma'am!" I replied proudly. "Bull shit!" she shouted, "I wouldn't vote for you if you was the last man alive!"

JOE McCARTHY

When the votes were counted, all the Democratic aspirants had been roundly defeated. But as 1951 dawned, I found more work to be done. Sen. Joe McCarthy was continuing to demagogue, and Wisconsinites were understandably uneasy about the way the world was going. Our young men had fought Hitler and Mussolini and Hirohito, but now Soviet-Chinese communism was threatening us everywhere. McCarthy had the easy answer: we were the victims of our own traitors—like Gen. George Marshall and Dean Acheson.

Clearly, we needed a strong Democratic candidate to tackle McCarthy in the 1952 election. But who? Young Bob La Follette, who had lost his Senate seat to McCarthy in the 1946 Republican primary, was still living in Washington. Bob had not campaigned effectively, and Joe, posing as "Tail Gunner Joe" the war hero, had won a narrow victory with the help of hundreds of votes from the communist-dominated auto workers' union at Allis-Chalmers in Milwaukee, the largest industry in the state. The auto workers had streamed into the open Republican primary to vote for McCarthy and against La Follette. Bob La Follette had been a staunch progressive in domestic policies and had outgrown earlier isolationist tendencies by helping my old boss, Averell Harriman, generate public acceptance for the Marshall Plan.

What if our new Democratic Party welcomed Bob into its ranks as our candidate and thus united the opposition to McCarthy? I invited Harriman, now back in Washington, to a lunch in Milwaukee to discuss the matter with about fifty other new Democrats, together with like-minded farm and labor leaders. The idea took hold at the meeting, and Harriman agreed to sound La Follette out about the possibility. This he did and reported that Bob seemed interested. So I flew to Washington and visited Bob in his office, where he represented Sears Roebuck (among other clients) as a lobbyist. He told me right off that, having weighed the matter, he felt he was not up to it. Not too long afterward this fine man took his life.

How was it, the political scientist may inquire, that the same Wisconsin voters who elected the admirable Old Bob La Follette could elect the destructive McCarthy? The answer, as best I can figure it out, is that both were plowing the same political soil, though with a harvest in view that was sincere for the former and cynical for the latter. That political soil had at least three ingredients.

The first was ethnic, to wit, pro-German. Wisconsin had a large population of German Americans and of Scandinavian Americans who at least through World War I felt allied with them. They believed they were being picked on, as indeed they sometimes were by wartime superpatriots. When Old Bob opposed World War I, though mainly on pacifist grounds, many of these ethnic groups saw him as coming to their rescue. By the time McCarthy came along, German Americans had two German-American wars in their memory books. They had been loyal Americans, but they longed for some suggestion that the Germans were not wholly at fault. This McCarthy supplied with a vengeance. Not only did he defend the SS massacres of U.S. prisoners at Malmédy as a frame-up, he smeared American war icons like Gen. George Marshall as little better than traitors.

The second ingredient was populist—government directly by the people. Old Bob had put on the statute books all the machinery of populism—the initiative whereby citizens may place a proposed law on the ballot, the referendum, and the recall of elected officials. McCarthy, while not much interested in these niceties of political science, distrusted and discredited representative government, preferring to leave government directly to "the people." Through regular elections representative government seeks to strike a delicate balance between majoritarian tyranny and elitist rule. The La Follettes and McCarthy came down hard on the populist side of the balance.

The third was conspiratorial. The La Follettes carefully constructed a gallery of enemies, from GOP bosses to eastern rail and grain interests. McCarthy was much more imaginative in his conspiracy invention, which included the Kremlin, most Democrats, Republican senators who did not kowtow to him, suspected Anglophiles like Secretary of State Dean Acheson, and homegrown traitors under every bush.

While the soil the La Follettes and McCarthy plowed so successfully for so long was similar, the harvests they reaped from it—the greatest good for the greatest number for the La Follettes, and his own cynical advancement for McCarthy—could not have been more different.

In an article I wrote for *Commonweal* in March 1962, called "Birch Bark, Birch Bite" (not a bad title for a piece jubilating that the right-wing John Birch Society lacked an economic program and was therefore fading), I suggested that Americans liked a fighter and that both La Follette and McCarthy filled the bill:

Much of their support came not only from the same population, but from the same attitudes in the population. The key is in their nicknames. La Follette to the day he died was "Fighting Bob." McCarthy in all the literature of the radical right is still referred to as "Fighting Joe." . . . Both took an aggressive, fighting stance in the political arena. To many voters both seemed fearlessly to be opposing enormous and mysterious powers.

The refusal of Bob La Follette, Jr., to run against McCarthy left the Democrats without a candidate just a year before the 1952 election. Several were flexing their muscles, but like the Keystone Kops of the early movies, they never moved. So I decided to take the plunge. "From now on, it's me or McCarthy" read the press release announcing my candidacy. I sent copies to friends throughout the country, asking for their comments and hoping for their support. One reply came from my old friend Carl McGowan, Gov. Adlai Stevenson's secretary and later a U.S. circuit judge: "Dear Henry, you have placed the voters of Wisconsin upon the horns of a delicious dilemma!"

So I was off to another campaign through my state's seventy-one counties. Starting off with a speech on the capitol steps in Madison, I laid into McCarthy and challenged him to sue me for libel if I, lacking his senatorial immunity, had spoken anything but the truth. I was conducting a negative campaign, but to this day I believe that was the only way to present the issue to the voters. For his part, McCarthy simply ignored me.

For eight months I campaigned as the apparent choice of the Democrats. I was pleased by the number of brave citizens who were willing to stick their necks out for me, at the risk of being denounced as communist sympathizers. One was the adorable Eppie Lederer (later to win fame as the columnist Ann Landers), who even enlisted the Catholic bishop of Eau Claire in my support.

In July 1952, on the last day for filing nomination papers, Tom Fairchild, who had been appointed U.S. attorney for the Western District of

Wisconsin at Madison after his 1950 defeat by Senator Wiley, suddenly announced his candidacy. In the weeks between his entry and the September primary, our race continued in a dead heat. I had the advantage of an early start and a corps of supporters who believed in me. Tom had the advantage of having been the first new Democrat to win, in 1948, the office of attorney general, and he had the strong support of the new DOC, which conveniently circulated his nomination papers. A further blow was that, as the primary approached, a number of labor leaders who had been firmly in my camp decided to hedge their bets by also endorsing Len Schmidt, a maverick Republican who was making headway against McCarthy in the Republican primary. This siphoned off some votes I was counting on.

On primary night Tom narrowly won. At a Democratic dinner in Milwaukee the next evening I offered him my full support. John Bunyan said it for me: "My sword I give to him who shall follow me in my pilgrimage."

But once again the Democrats were wiped out in the November election. McCarthy, many believe, might have been beaten had candidate Eisenhower, campaigning in Wisconsin, given the speech he had prepared, denouncing McCarthy and his tactics. Some powerful but unidentified Republican, it was said, must have talked Ike out of it. Some years later Wisconsin governor Walter Kohler, Jr., announced that *he* had warned off Ike. Asked to comment, I replied that this was tantamount to Kohler's boasting that he, rather than Mrs. O'Leary's cow, had started the Chicago fire.

The next year was a little better for me. Lowering my sights, I ran for the Milwaukee School Board in 1953 and won handily. I enjoyed my two years on the board, though my activities were mainly of a simple housekeeping nature rather than addressing broad matters of educational policy, which never seemed to surface. My fellow board members became friends and helped me in later races.

REAPPORTIONMENT, FLUORIDATION, AND "JOE MUST GO"

Early in 1953 grizzled old Fred Zimmerman, the Wisconsin secretary of state, asked me to represent him before the Wisconsin Supreme Court in the so-called reapportionment cases. He was challenging the legislature's habit of apportioning state senate and assembly districts to grossly favor rural over urban voters, thus ensuring a continuing conservative bias. The GOP, led by Governor Kohler, state chairman Wayne J. Hood, and Assemblyman Al Ludwigson of Waukesha County, were all vigorous adherents of the "areacrat" position. A little jingle I loved to recite summed it up:

> Votes should be based on butterfat
> Cried Ludwigson the areacrat.
> I'd go even farther than Ludwigson would

Said Republican chairman Wayne J. Hood.
If I have my way
(And I see it coming)
I'd base the vote on outdoor plumbing,
And every farmer with an old three-holer,
Could cast three votes for Governor Kohler.

We laughed all the way to the state's Supreme Court, where the areacrats were turned out and one-person-one-vote became the law in Wisconsin.

Another cause that quickened the spirit was the Milwaukee referendum on whether the city's water supply should be fluoridated. The scientific evidence, a group of us felt, showed that fluoridation was safe, inexpensive, and a real preventative of tooth decay, particularly for young children. Against the claim that we were tampering with the water supply, the referendum carried.

Still another, more important movement was in train. In 1953 Leroy Gore, a doughty Republican weekly editor from Spring Green, had started a "Joe Must Go" movement to acquire enough signatures on a petition to force McCarthy to face a recall special election. McCarthy had gone downhill since his 1952 reelection. Many Senate Republicans and even Ike himself were beginning to turn against his excesses. Gore obviously needed a broader base if his petition was to succeed. Eliot Walstead, Democratic state chairman, and I agreed that Gore deserved support. We succeeded in getting the Democratic state convention at La Crosse to endorse the proposal, and hundreds of Democrats soon joined Gore's signature seekers. But "Joe Must Go" failed to qualify with enough signatures, and the skirmish was lost. However, it made a dent in McCarthy, eroding his power in Washington until his censure and death four years later.

THE 1954 ELECTION

But 1954 was another election year, and it looked a little better for the Democrats. The year before, Lester Johnson, a Black River Falls Democrat, had won what had been a traditional Republican seat in northwestern Wisconsin. Moreover, Ike's economy was slowing down dramatically, and unemployment was increasing.

The Fifth District congressional seat in Milwaukee had been held by Republicans for most of the century. It was currently occupied by Charles Kersten, a McCarthy lieutenant, who had held it for six of the preceding eight years. Nonetheless, I felt that 1954 was my year, and I entered the race. My campaign would be based on a determination to improve the economy and on my opposition to the McCarthyism of my Republican opponent.

But first I had to dispose of Charley Greene, the Democratic Party chief in Milwaukee who had talked me out of running for lieutenant governor back in 1948. He entered the Democratic primary against me, denouncing me as "a banker in a Brooks Brothers suit." Greene went after me but appeared to the public as a voice from the past and got nowhere in the primary.

That left Kersten and a short October to campaign in. Because the Kersten campaign headquarters was in the old Liberty Theater, I couldn't help quoting Madame Roland during the French Revolution: "Ah Liberty! What crimes are committed in thy name!" Later that month Kersten's equally rabid colleague on the House Un-American Activities Committee, Michael Feighan of Ohio—and a Democrat to boot!—came to Milwaukee to give him a ringing endorsement. A few days later I got a friendly telegram from Mike Kirwan, also an Ohio Democrat and chair of the House Democratic Campaign Committee. He was sociably inquiring whether he could do any little thing to help me in the last days of the campaign. "Keep your boy friend Feighan out of Wisconsin" would have been an appropriate retort, but I was too busy to reply.

When the ballots were counted, I had won with 53 percent of the vote. Now, in the words of that ancient spiritual, I would be in that number when the saints went marching in. Six years of hard work and the refusal to let defeat defeat me—plus a bit of luck—had not been in vain.

Successive elections grew steadily easier. My first term saw an effort by the Republican legislature to redraw my district in order to add staunchly Republican Wauwatosa and subtract some Democratic strongholds. The bill passed the legislature, but Governor Kohler, to his credit, found it unconscionable and vetoed it. Never was I severely challenged thereafter, right up until my retirement in 1983. I had unpleasant primary battles in 1960, when I was weakened by my second unsuccessful run for the mayoralty, and in 1976, when my Democratic opponent flogged my prochoice stand on the abortion issue. Although I always campaigned hard—the Reuss coffee caravan covered almost every block in the district—my campaign expenditures were mercifully modest.

As a baby with Gustav Reuss, my grandfather, and Gustav Aldolph Reuss, my father

Astride my horse, Peggy, 1919

Amidst the ruins of Cologne, 1945

Enjoying a Wisconsin winter sport in Washington, D.C., 1955

On Horicon Marsh

Walking the Ice Age Trail

With my wife, Margaret, 1976

Part II

IN THE WELL
OF THE HOUSE
(1955–1983)

4

Foreign Policy

My apprenticeship in foreign affairs was well along before I arrived for the opening of the 84th Congress in January 1955. I had served in the war, with the military government in Germany, and had worked on the Marshall Plan. In 1950 I taught a course in foreign policy at what was then Wisconsin State College–Milwaukee and had gone on a lecture tour to Minneapolis, Des Moines, Tulsa, Little Rock, and points between to report on European reconstruction to local councils on foreign relations.

With this background I should have been an eager candidate for a seat on the House Committee on Foreign Affairs. But my Democratic colleague from Milwaukee, Clement J. Zablocki, had been installed on that committee since his arrival in 1948. So it would have been contentious as well as hopeless to have proposed myself. Thus I had to seek other ways of expressing my interest in world affairs.

THE COLD WAR

They were not long in coming. Secretary of State John Foster Dulles brought a stern and menacing presence to what had by now become the cold war. Any relationship between this august figure and an obscure first-term member of Congress from Wisconsin was bound to be negligible, and ours certainly was. Our only contact, if you can call it that, was when our little boys kicked their soccer ball into the neighboring Dulles backyard and were admonished by the Secret Service not to trespass again.

By 1955 Dulles had made his new hardline foreign policy apparent. He had inherited the major achievements of President Truman and Secretaries of State Marshall and Acheson—the Berlin airlift, the Marshall Plan, NATO. South Korea was again intact, as before the assault from the north. Not content with this legacy, Dulles speedily carried the cold war to every corner of the globe.

In Iran the Truman administration had refused to interfere with a revolution that had overthrown the shah and brought to power a regime under Mohammed Mossadegh that threatened to nationalize the British petroleum interests. But in 1953, under Dulles, the CIA joined with British Intelligence to organize a mob to overthrow Mossadegh and to restore the shah and the British oil company.

In 1954 a populist government in Guatemala under Jacobo Arbenz, planning to nationalize the U.S.-owned banana plantations, was overthrown by a right-wing military coup organized by, and with air support from, the CIA. Along the way Secretary Dulles was busy stitching together military alliances directed at what Dulles viewed as the Soviet-Chinese conspiracy throughout southeast Asia and the Middle East.

DULLES'S ONE-CHINA POLICY

The most threatening Dulles initiative was his one-China policy. Following the military defeat of Generalissimo Chiang Kai-shek by the communists and his retirement to Taiwan, Secretary of State Dean Acheson's policy had been to "let the dust settle." Not so with Dulles. Immediately, he articulated the one-China policy, whereby the generalissimo's government was recognized as ruler of all China, and the general himself was encouraged to return and conquer his lost mainland.

Thus the new overall Dulles cold-war foreign policy was highly militarized, adventurist, intent on pacts with doubtful allies. As I got to know the other first-term Democrats, I was not alone in concluding that the Dulles foreign policy required a debate.

THE FRESHMAN DEBATE

Shortly after I arrived in Washington I had met a very bright young historian-journalist named Sidney Hyman. He first suggested that I try to rally my new first-term Democratic colleagues to engage in a foreign policy debate some afternoon when no business was scheduled on the House floor. I found a lot of support for the idea from my new colleagues.

The result? A "freshman debate" occurred on March 10, 1955. As lead speaker, I made our central points—in Asia, an end to our support for the generalissimo's reconquest of mainland China; in Europe, disengagement involving a Soviet military withdrawal to Russia, and an Allied military withdrawal to the Rhine, with the security of the central European countries internationally guaranteed.

I suggested that President Eisenhower tell the world something along these lines:

We Americans want peace, and we want to do our part to secure the peace. . . .

To the people of Asia, Africa, and the Middle East, we say this. If you agree, we will ask the UN to take over Formosa as a trusteeship, to assume its defense against the aggression that threatens it, and to promote the development of self-government by the Formosan people. If you agree, we will work with you, both inside and outside the UN, for social and economic advancement, and against colonialism and feudalism.

To the people of Europe, we say this. If you agree, and if Russia will carry out her part of the bargain by withdrawing to her historic borders, we will welcome a unified and independent Germany; a free Poland, Czechoslovakia, Hungary, Austria, Romania, Bulgaria, and the Baltic States, each independent but part of a larger central European community based upon a respect for human rights; all without the capacity to make aggressive war, but with their security guaranteed by the UN.

To the people of all nations, we say this. We rededicate ourselves to work in humble hope with the rest of the world toward the goal of permanent peace, for our own continued survival is hinged to the prospect of permanent peace.

Acknowledging that this debate might be thought presumptuous by older members, Stewart Udall, the Arizona Democrat, observed that "if freshmen have any assets they can offer a body, it is usual that they have a little excess energy and occasionally a fresh point of view." Edith Green, Democrat of Oregon, urged a responsible program of foreign aid, lest we become "the richest man in the graveyard." Richard Lankford, Democrat of Maryland, agreed that the "policy of containment by military alliances is at best an expedient, a means to an end." James Roosevelt, Democrat of California, deplored that "we have by-passed, ignored, and half-heartedly supported the UN, a body established to promote world peace." James Quigley, Democrat of Pennsylvania, invoked his constituent, George F. Kennan, the author of the containment policy, as one who "would be the last to contend that containment was to become a permanent way of life." Charles Boyle, Democrat of Illinois, observed that "with the ground under us trembling from those recent atomic tests in Nevada, it is about time that a new generation add its little bit to retelling the age-old story that men everywhere believe in fellowship, in brotherhood, in peace under God."

Of course, there was disagreement as well. Republican Melvin Laird of Wisconsin forcefully rejected any attempt to disassociate ourselves from Chiang Kai-shek's mainland ambitions. Rotund "Tummy" Tumulty of New Jersey denounced his fellow Democratic first-termers as appeasers of communists "ready to drink blood from a skull."

Public reaction to the freshman debate was favorable. A number of leading newspapers had good things to say about our initiative. James Warburg, who had become a prolific author of books critical of current U.S. foreign policy, was so impressed that he shortly wrote a small book about the debate, *Turning Point Toward Peace* (1955). While welcome, the title clearly overstated things a bit. Richard Nixon did not go to China until 1972, bringing an end to the pretensions of Taiwan to govern the mainland. And

it was 1978 before the United States established formal diplomatic relations with the People's Republic. Shortly after "normalization," Sen. Lloyd
Bentsen, the Texas Democrat, and I led a Joint Economic Committee delegation on a memorable tour of China, the first such congressional venture.

DISENGAGEMENT IN EUROPE

As the 1950s advanced, I refined the concept of disengagement I had first
advanced in the 1955 freshman debate. In a June 1958 article in the *Commonweal* I spelled out why I believed that the West should propose an alternative to its policy of confronting Soviet forces eyeball to eyeball across the
iron curtain:

What the West needs is a policy that seeks an end to the nightmare of Eastern
Europe, a new order for those people whose hope for freedom in 1945 was dashed
by the designs of aggressive Communism, a policy which comes to grips with the
realities of our divided world, and which commends itself to the deep sense of justice which all people share.

What I proposed was a withdrawal of Russian troops to the Soviet Union's
historic boundaries and of British, French, and U.S. troops to the west
bank of the Rhine. Russia and NATO would guarantee free elections in
the Germanys, and foreign armies would withdraw from Middle Europe,
to which the West would pledge to work toward free elections and respect
for human rights. But was there the slightest chance that Russia would accept a settlement so advantageous to the West?

Let us assume that the chances of Russia's accepting the proposal are at present
close to nil. Is it nevertheless not important that the West lay before the World,
including Russia, a proposal that a reasonable and patriotic Russian, freed of mega-
lomaniac fantasies, might adopt?

Surely the proposal answers Russia's legitimate interests. It would reduce the
threat of an atomic war which Russia should want no more than we. . . . Russia
could conserve some of her strength for making the Russian people prosperous,
which, being human, they wish to be. Insurance against the setting-up of heavily
armed and hostile states on Russia's borders could provide a real measure of military security. And economic internationalism in Middle Europe would assure Russia of a trading area very much in her interest. . . .

Making a just proposal by the West is necessary even if we conclude that at the
moment there is no chance that the Russians will accept it. We cannot remain silent
on the kind of Middle Europe that we would like to emerge from the long nightmare of Communism. For, once known, our vision of a free, peaceful and humane
order in Middle Europe can begin to mold events. It can give encouragement to the
captive peoples. And it can hasten the day when more reasonable men can come to
power in Russia, by giving them, too, a goal.[1]

Some Europeans also were talking about disengagement. In Britain similar proposals were coming from Labourites like Hugh Gaitskell and Dennis Healey and Tories like Lord St. Oswald and in Germany from Social Democrats like Willy Brandt, independents like Wilhelm Schuetz (editor of *Aussenpolitik*), and Christian Democrats like Eugene Gerstenmaier.

In the end, those in power in the West rejected the idea of disengagement. I well remember the pundit Walter Lippmann's jumping all over me at a Washington dinner party for even suggesting something so outlandish. But if disengagement had been tried, would it have quickened the day of Russian withdrawal that finally came in 1990? Of such stuff are doctoral dissertations made.

For years I attempted to work out the theoretical underpinnings of an ideal U.S. foreign policy. I found it difficult to advance much beyond Abraham Lincoln's hope that our country be not the terror but the encourager of the world. With our mighty economic power, our rainbow coalition ethnically, our relative lack of classes socially, our democracy politically, and our sense of justice morally, we have a good base from which to project ourselves abroad. But this superpower base should be used not for throwing our weight around but rather for strengthening international organizations such as the UN.

My developing concept of a sensible foreign policy owed much to the teachings of a number of people I admired. I listened carefully to Sen. Bill Fulbright, the Arkansas Democrat, and his strictures against the arrogance of American power. I profited much from Democratic Montana senator Mike Mansfield's advice that, in searching for friends in the world, we should be less concerned with whether their government was a democracy like ours than whether it was reasonably humane.

Perhaps my most cherished mentor on foreign affairs was Benjamin Cohen. In his youth Ben and his sidekick, Tom Corcoran (Tommy the Cork, as FDR used to call him), had been the life of the New Deal. They wrote presidential speeches, drafted legislation like the Securities Act and the Public Utility Holding Company Act, and played the roles of court philosopher and jester. Now, a generation later, they were still in Washington. Corcoran had become a superlawyer-lobbyist who felt that he could burst into my office at any time with his clients' business. Cohen, on the other hand, continued in his autumn years to serve his gods of truth and justice. I could call day or night for his help. He had a strong belief in the possibilities of the United Nations, a firm grasp of the rule of law, and an appealing Socratic method of getting to the heart of the matter.

Before long I was forced to consider the question of military intervention by the United States. I was not dogmatically opposed to intervention. After all, I had participated in the biggest intervention of them all, World

War II, and I supported our Korean action, made easier because we fought under the banner of the United Nations. But what about all the rest?

A first case arose in July 1958, when President Eisenhower sent the marines into Lebanon, where the Christians and Muslims were warring. I rose on the House floor to criticize the incursion, urging that we invoke the United Nations and withdraw our troops as soon as possible. Speaker Sam Rayburn immediately stepped down from his dais to denounce criticism after our troops had landed. But Eisenhower shortly adopted what I suggested, invoked the UN, and withdrew our troops, without casualties to them or to the Lebanese. The same cannot be said of an identical landing in Lebanon under President Ronald Reagan a quarter-century later, with equal lack of justification and with vastly greater loss of American and Lebanese lives.

Shortly thereafter I developed for my own use a philosophical template for evaluating when military intervention was justified: Consider intervening only on behalf of a country or government that is reasonably humane, whose people are willing and able to bear their share of the burden, where our allies are favorably disposed, and where a vital U.S. interest is at stake.

These criteria would have negated intervention in just about every case in which it was attempted, and the world would have been better for it. The list would include the two Lebanons, the Bay of Pigs in 1961, Vietnam, Lyndon Johnson's intervention in the Dominican Republic, Nixon's in the parrot's beak of Cambodia, Gerald Ford's off the coast of Cambodia, Jimmy Carter's in the Iranian desert, Reagan's in Grenada, George Bush's in Panama, and Bill Clinton's in the Sudan.

THE PEACE CORPS

Foreign policy is usually the exclusive domain of the executive branch, but on rare occasions Congress can make a contribution. The Peace Corps was just such an occasion.

The idea for such a corps came to me in November 1957, as I traveled through the jungles of Cambodia. This was on a round-the-world tour by the Subcommittee on Foreign Operations, chaired by Porter Hardy, Democrat of Virginia, of my second committee, Government Operations. On that trip I had been put off by the giantism of our American aid programs. Huge steel mills, enormous dams, and international airports seemed to be what we did best. In Cambodia we inspected a new superhighway built with American dollars that stretched from the capital at Phnom Penh down to the Gulf of Tonkin. Its principal utility lay in its gravel shoulder, on which the peasants could walk their water buffaloes.

Later, back in Washington at dinner with Arnold Toynbee, I asked the venerable British historian of civilizations what he thought of the project.

"You know, Congressman," he replied, "often a mature civilization will build a highway from the capital out to where the barbarians lurk; but then the barbarians come down the highway and wipe out the civilization!" Something not unlike that later happened to poor Cambodia.

A few miles from this discouraging evidence in Cambodia I saw another activity that was wholly encouraging. Working their way through the jungle were four young Americans affiliated with International Volunteer Services, a nongovernmental organization that over the years has done many good things in far-off places. They were going from village to village setting up the first schools the countryside had known. They obviously loved their work, as the Cambodians loved their instruction.

I had their model in mind when, on returning to Washington, I began to put together what three years later was to become the Peace Corps. I made my youth corps proposal the subject of dozens of my speeches and articles, and I convened a series of meetings with leaders in business, labor, the clergy, and various voluntary organizations to hammer out a proposal for a more person-to-person approach to our foreign aid activities. I explained the proposed youth corps in an article in the *Commonweal*.

A Youth Corps would assure an adequate supply of young Americans to man public and private technical assistance missions in the years to come. But there are two even more important things to be said for it. Young Americans in their late teens and early twenties need a sense of purpose—the excitement and stimulus of taking part in great events. [As] William James pointed . . . out . . . a season on a fishing schooner or on a cattle ranch could well provide the sense of excitement and purpose which war—at least old-fashioned war—was supposed to provide. If the evolution of the have-not nations of Latin America, Asia, and Africa is at once the greatest challenge and adventure of the age, young Americans are going to want to become involved in it.

Furthermore, from the standpoint of a successful American foreign policy, a Youth Corps could be equally beneficial.

Too often we seem to emphasize military alliances with corrupt or reactionary leaders; furnishing military hardware which all too frequently is turned on the people of the country we are presumably helping; grandiose and massive projects; hordes of American officials living aloof in enclaves in the country's capital. Would we not be farther along if we relied more heavily on a group of some thousands of young Americans willing to help with an irrigation project, digging a village well, or setting up a rural school?[2]

Public response to the proposal was highly favorable. But the applause was not unanimous. Vice President Nixon called the idea a "haven for draft dodgers," and the *Chicago Tribune* ran an editorial entitled "Another Silly Idea from Congressman Reuss." Obviously, the Eisenhower administration would veto any attempt to actually enact any such program. But we thought of a strategy that might work—simply call for a study proposal as an amendment to the Mutual Security Act then making its way through Congress. Richard Neuberger, the Oregon Democrat who was to die a few weeks later, introduced the same amendment on the Senate side.

Our amendment carried, and the bill was signed into law on May 14, 1960. But the foreign appropriations bill still needed a line item to provide the government's share of the money to pay for the study. And, to our dismay, Rep. Otto Passman, a Louisiana Democrat who was a real enemy of progress, had the item stricken from the appropriations bill. Swallowing my pride, I went to see Passman and pleaded with him to restore the money. He said he would do so if I would promise to vote for *his* pet project, a campaign to eradicate the water lotus that was infesting his Louisiana bayous. I hope God will forgive me for consenting to this egregious piece of logrolling. At any rate, the appropriation passed in the summer of 1960, and the study started.

Candidate John F. Kennedy first proposed what was to become the Peace Corps in a campaign speech at the University of Michigan in Ann Arbor in September 1960. The idea had been passed on to him by Tris Coffin, editor of the *Washington Spectator*. As Coffin later explained it:

One day in 1960 Henry Reuss told me of his idea for an overseas service corps. I thought the idea was so good that it needed a national forum and debate. So I went to another friend, Senator Jack Kennedy, whom I had known ever since he was a lonely freshman congressman, and who was running for the presidency. He listened thoughtfully and when I had finished my spiel he said, "That's an interesting idea." Ten days later he gave his Peace Corps speech.[3]

With Kennedy's victory the Peace Corps became priority business. The study commissioned by our 1960 appropriation had been favorable. The new president was thus able to set up the corps within his first sixty days, even before the congressional authorization had been enacted. In his authorization request to Congress, Kennedy spoke of my bill and of a bill introduced later, in June 1960, by Sen. Hubert Humphrey of Minnesota, as the origin. By the summer of 1961 the first Peace Corps trainees were coming off the production line. I recall addressing an early class that had just been trained at the University of Wisconsin for an African mission: "You are leaving the Ivory Tower for the Ivory Coast!"

Throughout the 1960s and after, I made it my business to spend some time in the field with the Peace Corps whenever I could. In Senegal with my friend, then-representative Andy Young, Democrat of Georgia, we visited a little village where the Peace Corps had built a well.[4] In Chile I spent a week with Peace Corps volunteers in a rural school—long enough to get used to the water, and my internal economy quieted down. All around the globe—in Kenya, the Philippines, Laos, Colombia, Peru, Panama—I saw

Peace Corps volunteers putting a human face on the U.S. presence and in return acquiring what James called the "toughness without callousness . . . [that is] the moral equivalent of war."

For me, the Peace Corps was shortly to have a German sequel. In April 1961 Speaker John McCormack called me to his office to meet a visitor from Germany, Walter Casper of Frankfurt, a director of Metalgesellschaft, the huge metallurgical firm. Like the Speaker, Walter was an ardent Catholic and a believer in the social teachings of the Sermon on the Mount. He had heard about the Peace Corps and felt it might be just what the new Germany, still trying to find itself after the Hitler days, needed. Would I be willing to visit Germany to help set up a German version of the Peace Corps? With the Speaker's encouragement, I said yes.

That summer I followed through on my promise. I was accompanied by two stars from Marquette University, Dr. Erich Waldheim, a political scientist of German origin, and Brother Leo Ryan, a jolly friar from the School of Business Administration. Both had become enthusiastic about the Peace Corps and jumped at the chance to play some part in it. We spent several weeks visiting in every major West German city with leading people from government, business, labor, the churches, and the universities. By the time we left, there was general agreement that a FriedensKorps very much on the Peace Corps model should be established as soon as possible. Foreign Minister Heinrich von Brentano, signed a document ordaining such a corps, virtually his last act before he retired and soon died.

Back in Washington, I was kept abreast of progress in the Bundesrepublik of the new German peace corps. But sadly, because of bureaucratic delay, progress was agonizingly slow. The year 1962 passed, and now it was May 1963, and there was still no German peace corps. Then, in mid-May, Kennedy called me to the White House. As we sat on the second-floor veranda overlooking the Ellipse, he told me that he planned to visit Germany in June and asked me, his informal political adviser on Germany (I had headed up his German American campaign group in the 1960 election), what suggestions I might care to make. I suggested three things, all of which were ultimately included. The first was a visit to the historic Paulskirche in Frankfurt, where the abortive German Parliament had sat in 1848 as it tried to set up a democratic government. Unfortunately, as somebody said, "The German people can never make a revolution; the police will not allow it!"

The second was one everyone agreed on: go to Berlin and make a speech in front of the wall that the communists had just built. Kennedy's "Ich bin ein Berliner" speech went down in history as one that sustained hopes of freedom for the next thirty years, until freedom finally came. Later, Kennedy detractors claimed that, to Germans, a Berliner is a jelly roll and that Kennedy's assertion that he was a jelly roll elicited chuckles, not cheers, from his audience. But the recording of the speech shows this is a canard; besides, a Berliner is a jelly roll only in Hamburg, not in Berlin.

My third recommendation, somewhat sly, had to do with the Peace Corps. The Germans were about to adopt his baby, I told the president, and with a little luck there might be a photo opportunity there. "Great!" he said, "I'll have Sarge [Shriver, our Peace Corps director] call the German embassy and we'll get this started." The request, I've been told, caused some initial consternation at the German embassy in Washington and in Bonn. But there must have been a flurry of activity, because when the president arrived in June a contingent of clean-cut young Germans was ready for their FriedensKorps mission. My friend Walter Casper looked on delightedly as the president reviewed them.

CUBA

The populous island republic of Cuba kept bobbing up on my radar screen. We had maintained relations with the corrupt and tyrannical Batista dictatorship in Havana right up until his ouster by the revolutionary forces of Fidel Castro in 1957. But the Eisenhower administration's initial toleration of Castro steadily evaporated, until in January 1961, a few days before leaving office, Ike formally broke off diplomatic relations with Castro. Just one member of Congress raised a protest—me. In a CBS television interview I made my case that as long as we recognized the Soviet Union and other communist states, it made no sense to single out our neighbor Cuba for oblivion. It would be preferable to maintain relations and by diplomacy attempt to work for better things.

Matters only worsened. There ensued the abortive Bay of Pigs invasion; the Cuban missile crisis of 1962 in which President Kennedy showed a level head; numerous amateurish attempts by the CIA to assassinate Castro; and thirty-five years of nonrecognition, which have had the sole effect of solidifying Castro in his position on the island.

During a brief interlude of sanity under Carter, we established a U.S. interests mission in Havana and were on our way to reaching a more sensible relationship with the beleaguered island. In 1978 I led a bipartisan delegation of the House Banking, Housing, and Urban Affairs Committee to Cuba and had a four-hour interview with Castro. Almost the whole first hour was taken up with personal pleasantries that reflected an excellent intelligence briefing by the Castro team: did I enjoy duck hunting, and what was it like on Lake Winnebago? In the lagunes of Cuba we have to sneak up on the ducks like this. We pledged to invite each other to go shooting on Lake Winnebago or in the lagunes at some future date. Ending this Hemingwayesque episode, I brought the conversation around to what might be done to improve relations between our two countries. "End your embargo, recognize our Afro-Latin character, and all will be well," was the best I could get. As I write, our position toward Cuba has, if anything, worsened. Unless we change our policy, Cuba after Castro may be the next in line for a repetition of Yugoslavia after Tito.

VIETNAM

Vietnam was surely the saddest chapter in the history of our country during my congressional years. It turned LBJ from the triumphant prince of civil rights legislation, Medicare, the War on Poverty, and activist government in general into the tragic victim of his own hubris. It tore apart the Democratic Party. It ruined any chance that Hubert Humphrey might have had to lead the nation. It embittered a whole generation of young Americans against their society. It prefaced the ending of the golden age of good government.

Uneasy about Vietnam from the beginning, I salved my conscience, alone or in company with likeminded colleagues, by endless visits to administration leaders to plead for withdrawal and by numerous speeches and debates. A debate at the Marquette University Union with my House colleague Clement Zablocki, a Vietnam hawk, caused him to be described in the next day's newspaper story as a "gentle hawk" and me as a "belligerent dove." By no means a gentle hawk was columnist Joe Alsop, who announced to a startled group at a Washington dinner table that when we won the war in Vietnam, I would be among the first to be hanged.

Nothing seemed to make a dent on the administration. Our one-time hero, Vice President Hubert Humphrey, came back from a Vietnam trip in 1967 to tell a group of House Democratic doubters in a meeting in the Speaker's dining room that we shouldn't be beguiled into thinking that Hanoi was a fine group of liberals along the lines of Americans for Democratic Action. This we found insulting, and we left the room shaking our heads.

Then, in late 1967, came the surprise entry of Sen. Eugene McCarthy of Minnesota into the race for the 1968 Democratic presidential nomination. Gene had been a close friend of mine in the House and a cofounder of the Democratic Study Group. Soon his candidacy was endorsed by my Wisconsin Democratic colleague Bob Kastenmeier, then by my wife, Margaret. So, in early January 1968, proclaiming that "a family that endorses together, stays together," I joined in this rebellious endorsement.[5]

McCarthy's surprisingly good showing in the New Hampshire primaries frightened the White House. As I campaigned for "Clean Gene" throughout Wisconsin, I perceived that he was going to win the primary against LBJ. People viewed the primary as a sort of referendum on Vietnam, and here at last was an opportunity to express themselves. A trusted administration lieutenant, Les Aspin, then at the Department of Defense, was dispatched to Wisconsin to report on the probable results of the early April Wisconsin primary. He reported correctly that LBJ was in deep trouble. LBJ, heeding the report, announced two days before the primary that he would not be a candidate.

Now McCarthy was acquiring some competition for his role as the anti-Vietnam Democratic candidate. Bobby Kennedy, whose energy and passion I had come to admire greatly, entered the race. This looked like a disaster: two anti-Vietnam candidates running against the LBJ-anointed Humphrey at the convention could only result in a Humphrey victory. I dispatched a telegram to Gene, my candidate, and to Bobby: would they be willing to sit down together to discuss whether their candidacies might be sorted out in order to avert such an outcome? Bobby replied that he would be willing; I never heard from Gene, and so nothing came of the proposal.

I continued my campaigning for Gene, even to Oregon and Alaska. Then came Bobby's assassination on the night of the California primary. As the Chicago convention approached, it became apparent that Gene would lack the votes to defeat his one-time Minnesota ally, Hubert Humphrey. We scattered anti–Vietnam War advocates were determined to seek at least a strong antiwar plank in the party platform. I took part in that debate, urging the delegates:

We made our mistake when we sent a land army into Vietnam. The Saigon government has denied the right to free elections. It has sent to jail for five years the runner-up in the last presidential election because he advocated compromise. We must not now give Saigon our proxy to conduct the foreign policy of the United States. We must not give them a blank check that we shall have to honor with American lives and American treasure.

We must find our way and say: there shall be no more Vietnams!

But we lost the fight for the minority end-the-war plank. The day before the vote on the platform I ran into my old friend Ken Galbraith on the convention floor. Like me, he was a disheartened supporter of Gene McCarthy's. Was there any hope for the presidency, we asked each other, now that Gene had for all practical purposes been counted out and now that Bobby Kennedy was gone? What if young Ted Kennedy, waiting in Massachusetts, appeared in Chicago to lead the fight for the antiwar plank? (This was a year before Chappaquiddick.) If the plank lost, no harm would be done. If the plank carried, the resulting antiwar momentum might just be enough to propel Teddy to the nomination and then on to win the election. But Teddy declined, the strategy evaporated, and we shall never know whether history might have been changed.

In November the Republicans, led by Richard Nixon and Spiro Agnew, won narrowly, and the Vietnam War continued for another seven years.[6]

Nixon's invasion of Cambodia in April 1970 was the reason for the protest at Ohio's Kent State University in which national guardsmen killed four students and wounded nine. Demonstrations soon spread to about 350 college campuses. When police killed two students and wounded twelve at Jackson State College in Mississippi, I flew down with Democratic senator Ed Muskie of Maine and others to try to restore calm. Shortly after, when the chancellor at the University of Wisconsin–Madison asked me to address a campus antiwar rally, I agreed. My message to the students: my outrage is as great as yours, but the remedy is not to burn down your alma mater. They didn't.

Glimpses of Lyndon Johnson over the years reinforced the view that his was a truly tragic figure. Bigger than life, he was brought down by a Texas sense of patriotism, which saw in Vietnam another Alamo.

Under Eisenhower, Johnson had run the Democratic Senate with magisterial skill. He knew how to wheedle and cajole his committee chairmen into harmony. His powerful leadership soon dismayed Bill Proxmire, the Wisconsin Democrat then serving his first term in the Senate (this was 1957). Prox tilted in vain against the king, with no more effect than a swallow swooping low over a summer's pond.

Johnson smarted under the second-class treatment he thought he received as Kennedy's vice president. Flying to Milwaukee from Washington on Air Force Two for a speech at the state Democratic convention in 1962, Johnson spent almost the whole ninety minutes complaining to us of the Kennedy brothers' ill treatment of him. He was raring to go, he felt, but was not being given a chance.

Johnson could be autocratic. I remember the 1966 case of Abba Schwartz, a State Department official in charge of sensitive immigration matters and a protégé of Eleanor Roosevelt's. For some reason, he fell afoul of Secretary of State Dean Rusk, who fired him. Asked to comment by a *New York Times* reporter, I said that Schwartz had been doing a good job and didn't deserve to be sacked. The story appeared above the fold in the next morning's *Times*. That afternoon I arrived at the White House for a bill signing. As I approached LBJ to receive my pen, he growled at me: "Henry, I wish you'd stop trying to get your name in the paper before you know what you're talking about; see Rusk and find out about this fellow Schwartz." I wish I could report that I waved aside the pen and told the president what he could do with it. Instead, I took it meekly, went to see Dean Rusk the next day, and over a bourbon and branch water listened to his unconvincing reasons for getting rid of Schwartz. Of such stuff are heroes not made.

LBJ could also be devious. I spent hours with him one summer's night in 1967 on the front porch of the Lake Barcroft, Virginia, home of Barefoot Sanders, a bright and charming Texan who had become Johnson's congressional liaison. We were discussing LBJ's proposal for a general income tax hike to help pay for the Vietnam War, which he knew I opposed. I urged on him instead a much fairer way to raise whatever revenues were needed—plug some of the loopholes riddling our income tax laws. My list of loopholes of course included the oil depletion allowance, to Texans a sacred flame never to be extinguished. Without mentioning oil, LBJ flooded me with reasons that made closing loopholes impossible.

Soon came my break with him over Vietnam, his decision not to run, and his retirement to his Texas ranch. I saw him once again—at the 1972 funeral at the New Orleans cathedral for Rep. Hale Boggs, the Democrat killed in an Alaskan plane crash. LBJ and I had a long talk in the presbytery as we waited for the service to begin. Although he told me his end was approaching—he did in fact die within weeks—he graciously overlooked my apostasy as we remembered the glory days in 1964 and 1965. Once again he seemed bigger than life.

GREECE

Another sorry chapter in our foreign policy was our acquiescence in the ouster by a right-wing military junta of the democratically elected government of Greece. The junta, with U.S. help, ruled Greece as a military dictatorship from 1967 to 1974.

What the United States should have done when army officers took over in Greece is what the Clinton administration did with a similar dictatorship in Haiti—oppose the military and work to restore the democratically elected government. This should especially have been the policy with respect to Greece, the cradle of democracy and our ally in a NATO whose purpose was to preserve democracy. For reasons that were mysterious at the time, the Nixon administration vigorously supported the junta from 1969 on and discouraged those patriotic Greeks who were trying to restore democratic rule.

A little band of House Democrats—Ben Rosenthal of New York, John Brademas of Indiana, Don Fraser of Minnesota, me, and others—did what we could to counter Nixon's involvement with the junta. But we could do little but educate the public about what our government was perpetrating.

My small role was to use what little power I had as chair of an obscure banking subcommittee on foreign aid. We got word that the Nixon administration was making a substantial grant to a junta development agency headed by an economist who some years earlier had been caught plagiarizing the doctoral dissertation of a colleague at the University of Toronto. I convened a hearing of our subcommittee to look into the prudence of entrusting U.S. taxpayers' dollars to a professor who had swiped a colleague's dissertation and thus might be tempted to swipe some of our tax dollars. Livingston Merchant, head of the Nixon administration's aid program, indignantly denied that the professor had any such tendency.

Sadly, our government kept right on supporting the junta, until the junta invaded Cyprus in 1974, and the Greek people themselves tossed the junta out and restored democracy. A full explanation of the Nixon administration's extraordinary involvement with the junta finally emerged with the publication of the Nixon tapes in October 1997. In March 1973 Nixon was looking for hush money in order to keep the Watergate burglars from implicating him. He got the cash from Thomas Pappas, a wealthy Greek American with close ties to the junta, in return for a promise of Nixon's continuing help for the junta. On March 2, 1973, H. R. Haldeman told Nixon that Pappas was providing the hush money in return for Nixon's support.

NIXON: Good. I understand. No problem. . . . How's he [Pappas] doing?
HALDEMAN: Apparently he's sort of one of the unknown J. Paul Gettys of the world right now.
NIXON: Great. I'm just delighted.

On March 7 Nixon was thanking Pappas in the Oval Office:

NIXON: I want you to know that . . . I'm aware of what you're doing to help out in some of these things. . . . I won't say anything further, but it's very seldom you find a friend like that, believe me.

Shortly after the junta fell, I found myself in Athens to give a talk at the National Bank of Greece, headed by my old friend Xenophon Zelotas. An opponent of the junta, he had kept his integrity during the dark years. As I looked out at a parade of thousands of Athenians who were celebrating their liberation from the junta in Constitution Square, it was good to see the cradle of democracy rocking again.

TOWARD A CONCERT OF THE DEMOCRACIES

From the 1960s on I saw the need for a new, single, strong international organization composed of the major industrialized democracies and dedicated to the sensible economics and democratic politics that we saw as our world objective.

The UN was a jewel, but its universality, approaching two hundred nations today, makes it an inadequate vehicle for encouraging democracy. The UN needs to repair its exclusion of Germany and Japan from permanent Security Council membership, which their stature deserves. It needs to create an efficient command-and-control structure and an effective military force for its peace-keeping function. Above all, an overwhelmingly pro-UN public opinion ought to be brought to bear on a deadbeat Congress to pay our arrears in dues.

Though it has served its military purpose well, NATO lacks any real political or economic dimension. Because the main problems of the collapsed Soviet empire are political and economic rather than military, the countries of eastern Europe need a political and economic connection with us rather than a military one. Thus our recent preoccupation with enlarging NATO, a military organization, rather than creating a meaningful new political-economic organization, seems wrongheaded.

The cold war did see the formation of at least five, largely duplicating and increasingly obsolete, international political-economic organizations—the G-7 or -8, with its annual photo-opportunity summit meetings; the Organization for Economic Cooperation and Development, with a broad membership from Europe, North America, and Japan—Australia-New Zealand; the UN's Economic Commission for Europe; the Organization on Security and Cooperation in Europe, which lacks membership by Japan–Australia–New Zealand; and the all-European Council of Europe.

With responsibility dispersed to five separate agencies, it is no wonder that the leading market-oriented democracies, of which so much was expected, have proved unable to coordinate their political and economic policies, much less address constructively the problems of the formerly communist lands and of the developing world. To that end, the new organization would need to reform the International Monetary Fund and the World Bank into a new world financial institution capable of exercising on an international scale something approaching the monetary powers of our Federal Reserve, the regulatory powers over financial institutions of our Securities and Exchange Commission, and the examining powers of our federal banking agencies. To work, free markets need supervision, both at home and abroad.

I have long said that what we need is a merger of these five obsolete and ineffective organizations into one strong new one.[7] Democracy should be a requirement of membership in the new organization, a characteristic of its procedures, and a goal of its activities; hence the name, Concert of the Democracies (see Chapter 3). Its members could initially include those members of the five organizations that prove themselves democratically inclined, economically modern, and eager to cooperate internationally.

The world political goal of such a new organization would be fair elections, honest courts, competent bureaucracies, and the rule of law. It is tempting to speculate what the situation in the former Yugoslavia would be today had a strong political organization of the industrialized democracies existed before the breakup started. What if such an organization had insisted that post-Tito Yugoslavia couple its commendable record in suppressing fratricidal ethnic conflict with a good-faith effort to introduce rudimentary democratic practices, as Poland and Hungary were doing? What if the organization had restrained its members from prematurely recognizing the fragments of a dismembered Yugoslavia, pending a humanitarian solution? We shall never know.

The concert's economic goal would be to coordinate its members' fiscal, monetary, financial, trade, aid, labor, energy, and environmental policies, for their own good and that of the developing world.

Such an organization would cure the problem-solving failings of the five organizations we have today by incorporating the heads of the G-8 governments, ready for a summit meeting at least once a year. It would rid the G-8 of its Cinderella character by equipping it with a permanent staff. The G-8 powers might well operate as a caucus or steering committee within the larger organization.

The concert would give Japan, Australia, and New Zealand a more prominent institutional role in addressing the problems of the formerly communist states. Japan cannot be expected to assume a role in Europe that is consistent with its economic importance if Japan has no place at the table. Australia and New Zealand would bring to the concert both a history of involvement in Europe's wars and examples of thriving democracies.

As for Europe's formerly communist countries, the concert would give them an interim lodging that meaningfully addressed their political and economic problems, pending their admission to the European Union.

This organization could give the United States a responsible European role that is less egocentric than our present preoccupation with expanding NATO, an organization dominated by the United States. For a change, we would be placing our bets on the right horse.

Fifty years ago America created new institutions to deal with the challenge of a new postwar world. Today's post–cold war world challenges us to create a new political-economic institution of comparable grandeur.

5

The Environment

Wisconsin is the state of clean air, sparkling water, and an enchanting earth shaped by the glaciers of ages past. It is also the state of John Muir, the father of our national parks, and of Aldo Leopold, the protagonist of modern ecology. The trail from Muir's boyhood home, along the Fox River, over the portage, and up the Wisconsin River to Leopold's Sand County shack is to a Wisconsonite what the Via Sacra was to the ancient Romans.

What happy memories I have of hiking and skiing in the Kettle Moraine (a moraine is a long ridge left by the lobes of a glacier); crouching in a duck blind at Poygan, Puckaway, Butte des Morts, Horicon, or Winnebago; wading in a central Wisconsin trout stream; sailing a Snipe on a Waukesha County lake in summer or skate-sailing in winter.

So I came to Congress as a passionate environmentalist. But my major committee assignment, the Banking and Currency Committee, seemed to offer little connection to the outdoors.

WATERFOWL AND GRAIN

This proved not entirely the case. In April 1955 the assistant secretary of the interior for fish and wildlife wrote an article in the *Saturday Evening Post* about the troubles he was having with the San Francisco bankers. It seems that they were avid duck hunters and that they insisted on scattering grain in front of their duck blinds in order to attract the great flights of ducks and geese that migrate south every autumn. Now, "baiting" had been illegal for many years, an unsportsmanlike way to endanger further the continent's fragile waterfowl population. But instead of enforcing the law, the assistant secretary confessed that he found the bankers very difficult and so just looked the other way. I thought that this attitude was indefensible for a prominent official. So I made a speech on the House floor demanding that he enforce the law. He chose instead to resign. His successor saw to it that the department no longer winked at baiting.

However, stopping the scattering of grain in front of hunting blinds still left a problem. As the waterfowl migrated from the Arctic to the tropics, they frequently encountered shortages of natural food in the resting refuges the government had provided along the route. Why should they die for lack of grain when the government's Commodity Credit Corporation had millions of tons of wheat and corn, purchased to protect farm prices, in its silos? Here was an obvious serendipity: use some of this grain before it spoiled to feed exigent ducks and geese. To make matters easier, my Banking and Currency Committee had jurisdiction, for some mysterious reason, over the Commodity Credit Corporation. So it took little time to introduce my bill, get it favorably reported out of the banking committee, and passed in the House. In the Senate I enlisted the aid of the crusty old conservative Democrat who chaired the Senate Banking and Currency Committee, Willis Robertson of Virginia, father of today's evangelical Pat Robertson. The senator, an enthusiastic duck hunter, was easily persuaded, and the bill became law. So far, I seemed to be linking banking and wildlife with some success.

Later, in 1962, I secured passage of legislation prohibiting the use of federal funds to subsidize the drainage of wetlands. This ended the Department of Agriculture's practice in the 1950s of helping destroy wetlands essential to the survival of the nation's waterfowl.

THE MENOMINEE

During the congressional recess in the summer of 1955, I took my two little boys on an "inspection trip" of Wisconsin that included a swim in John Muir's Fountain Lake in Marquette County, a helicopter ride at Camp McCoy, and a visit to the land of the Menominee Indians northwest of Green Bay.

These "first persons"—the Menominee—had received forked-tongue treatment at the hands of white Americans. At the treaty of the Wolf River in 1853, duly executed between President Franklin Pierce and Chief Oshkosh, the tribe was promised a large part of Wisconsin because of its ancestral claim. But the Menominee were soon forced back into the small enclave that they occupy today—a beautiful forest of virgin white pine and hemlock, unspoiled lakes, and swift-flowing streams.

So things went until 1953, the first year of the Eisenhower administration. The Menominee had sued the federal government for its mismanagement of their forest and had won a substantial judgment. But in 1953 Congress passed the Menominee Termination Act, stipulating that the tribe could collect its judgment only if it agreed to end its reservation status and become "privatized" (without federal support).

During our 1955 visit my newfound Menominee friends told me of their worries. The forest, managed on a sustained-yield basis (so that the harvest is replaced by regrowth), and its sawmill were their principal means of livelihood. They feared that one day a lumber company would buy up the forest from the individual tribal members who now owned it and proceed to clearcut it. They showed me Spirit Rock, at the falls of the Wolf River, and told me of the legend that when it splintered, the tribe would disintegrate too.

Together we prepared an amendment to the 1953 Termination Act that mandated that the forest be managed forever on a sustained-yield basis. With friends on both the House and Senate Interior Committees, we were able to get the bill enacted into law. The Menominee have had their problems in the years since, but the forest—and Spirit Rock—still stand.

This bill to save the Menominee forest, and the earlier two to protect migratory waterfowl, were my main legislative victories in the environmental arena during my first five years, when I served under a Republican administration. This record of bill passing is less than epochal, but my aim under a hostile administration was to establish a public position, not primarily to pass bills. (In late 1969, when I decided to run for mayor of Milwaukee, my opponent, Henry Maier, attacked my environmental record in Congress as "one for the Indians and two for the birds." All I could do was sputter.)

Though the Menominee forest was now protected, the tribe was still very poor. Housing was miserable, often only tar-paper shacks. The new Kennedy administration was hospitable to local needs. With a team from the Washington housing agencies, I sat down with the Menominee and worked out a plan for forming the Menominee County Housing Authority. The new authority, with some federal help, was able to build livable ranch-style homes made of Menominee lumber, at affordable rents, in about three years. They still stand.

It was possible to help the Menominee in other ways—their schools, their health services, and a long-range economic development plan. I soon saw that they needed a political organization as well. Surely they deserved a unit of the new up-and-coming Wisconsin Democratic Party. So I asked Jim Megellas, state Democratic director, to come to Menominee country with me for a meeting with any Native Americans who might like to join the party. Classically handsome, Megellas was from a Greek American family in Fond du Lac that had known hard times during the depression. Young Jim remembered picking up stray coal along the Soo Line railroad tracks to keep the family going. Jim went on to a career in our foreign aid service. Amazingly, Sparky Waukau, the Menominee leader who was shortly elected chairman of the new county Democratic Party, was a dead ringer for Megellas—both handsome as Apollo, wise as Solon. Sparky devoted a long life to the welfare of his tribal brothers and sisters.

THE POTOMAC

I fell in love with the Potomac early on. This mighty river drained the Appalachian Mountains and descended from the Piedmont to tidewater at Great Falls just above the District of Columbia. George Washington and Thomas Jefferson had so treasured this magical stream that they agreed to Alexander Hamilton's demand that the U.S. Treasury assume the debts of the Continental Congress in return for Hamilton's allowing the new capital to be located on the Potomac.

By the early 1950s the great river was in danger. The Army Corps of Engineers wanted to build a series of huge dams on the upstream Potomac and its tributaries to hold back the ever-threatening floodwaters. The highway authorities wanted to build a superhighway 180 miles long, from Washington up to Cumberland, Maryland, along the site of the abandoned Chesapeake and Ohio Canal. The canal had been dug in the 1830s, just in time to see the new railroads make it obsolete. The barges had ceased operating in the 1920s, but the wondrous locks, towpaths, bridges, and tunnels remained.

Fortunately, in the spring of 1954 a doughty group coalesced, determined to save the Potomac from the dams and highways. Its leader was Supreme Court Justice William O. Douglas. Bill Douglas, from the state of Washington, had brought an expansive doctrine of the public interest both to Supreme Court jurisprudence and to nature. These hardy folk hiked the 180 miles, calling public attention to the danger to the national heritage. The would-be builders of dams and highways retreated, and the towpath was saved forever as the C&O National Scenic Trail.

When I arrived in Washington the next year, I immediately got aboard Bill Douglas's juggernaut. Every spring we would hike a segment of the trail, for our own enjoyment and as a signal that we were still on patrol. Once, thirsty and grimy after a long day's hike, Bill Douglas; Sen. Paul Douglas, the Illinois Democrat; and I hobbled into the stylish canalside patio of the Angler's Inn, just downstream from Great Falls, and asked for water. The maître d', sensing a threat to property values, gently told us to move on. "No room for them at the inn," headlined the Washington papers the next day.

Another Potomac mentor in my early days was my colleague in the 84th Congress, Rep. John Dingell, Democrat of Michigan. An ardent hunter and outdoorsman, John took me on as a hunting partner and as cosponsor of various projects to save the Potomac.

Dyke Marsh was a resting place for migrating ducks just down the river from National Airport. A sand and gravel company was about to get a permit from the Army Corps of Engineers to scoop up this nearby wilderness and carry its sand and gravel off to be used on some new highway. Dingell and I protested to the corps, and the gravel company was told to look elsewhere. Dyke Marsh survives to this day. Dingell went on to become a power in the House, rightly respected for his achievements in conservation and in energy. If at times he seemed too close to the Detroit automobile manufacturers, or to the National Rifle Association, his accomplishments far outweighed these flaws.

The next assault upon the Potomac occurred upstream. Near the battle-field of Antietam a utility company in 1967 proposed to build an unsightly power line for miles along the river's bluff. Working with the Maryland and Virginia regulatory agencies, we persuaded the utility to modify its plans. The vista was preserved.

One more threat to the Potomac presented itself. Hunting Towers was a large upscale apartment complex on the shores of Hunting Creek where it joins the Potomac just south of Alexandria, Virginia. In the late 1960s the owners of that complex applied to the Army Corps of Engineers for a permit to fill in the Potomac to create the land on which to construct addi-tional apartments—a nice way of avoiding having to pay for the needed land. The corps signaled that it would grant the fill permit.

Obviously, if anyone who wanted inexpensive land could just fill in the river, the Potomac would shortly become a narrow ditch as it flowed past the nation's capital. But how to convince the corps that a fill per-mit was not in the public interest? I discovered a couple of things. One was that Hunting Towers apartments, in its tenant selection, discriminated racially: black Americans, in those days before fair housing laws, were simply turned down by Hunting Towers's management. My second dis-covery was that George Washington, on a stroll from his nearby Mount Vernon, was wont to walk the very shores now proposed for landfill. An antifill coalition swiftly formed between the NAACP, which opposed the discrimination, and the Daughters of the American Revolution, which op-posed the desecration. When I testified at the corps hearing at Alexandria City Hall, I called the examiner's attention to the forging of this unlikely coalition. The permit was denied.

In the 1970s our family connection with the Potomac deepened. Mar-garet's friend Beth Kent had for some years owned Minnie's Island, a ten-acre islet just downstream from Great Falls. This leafy wilderness just twenty minutes from the Capitol had a shack on its highest rock that had resisted every flood. When Beth grew too old to navigate out to the island, Margaret and our son Christopher acquired Minnie's from her. We and our friends used it joyously for twenty years until we too found navigation difficult. In 1994 Margaret gave the island to Potomac Conservancy, which is preserving its natural character.

TRIPS TO GERMANY AND SWEDEN

One learns by travel, I have always held, and this is particularly true of eco-travel. So it was that in 1962 I visited Germany on an environmental search. Our waterways had recently become particularly troubled by the phosphate detergents widely used in America's washing machines. Although phosphate detergents were far from being the most threatening of our water pollutants, they did produce unsightly masses of foam as their residues reached the waterways. The Germans had both the problem and the solution, I was told. The problem was evident when I visited Heidelberg on the Neckar and there saw, where the fictional Student Prince once strolled, a huge Niagara of detergent foam. The solution became evident at the German Institute for Water, Earth, and Air near Bonn on the Rhine—find a way to make detergents that will clean without foaming. I carried the idea back home, where ultimately the detergent industry replaced the trouble-making phosphates.

In the early seventies I was invited by the Swedish government to join a group of a dozen environmentalists from as many countries to look at Sweden's advances in environmental protection. We traveled from Stockholm to Göteborg to Malmö, viewing the latest technological breakthroughs in waste treatment, biodegradable substances, and pollution-free farming. At journey's end someone suggested a limerick contest to celebrate our adventure. My entry received an honorable mention:

> At a waste-water works in Malmö
> Cried a lusty young worker named Bö:
> Biologic demand
> Has got quite out of hand;
> I'm dying to carnally knö.

THE CONSERVATION SUBCOMMITTEE

By the mid-1960s I had acquired enough seniority on my second committee, the Government Operations Committee, to be eligible for a subcommittee of my own, which I speedily called the Subcommittee on Conservation and Natural Resources. The subcommittee proved to be a real tiger. With John Moss of California and Bella Abzug of New York on the Democratic side, and moderates Gilbert Gude of Maryland, Pete McCloskey of California, and Guy Vander Jagt of Michigan on the Republican side, we had the time of our lives.

Through our 1971 hearings we put pressure on the Department of Agriculture's Soil Conservation Service (SCS) to stop its insensate "channelizing" of streams.

Our subcommittee took a field trip down to the nearby Gilbert Swamp in southern Maryland. The Soil Conservation Service had been at work.

Where a lazy river had meandered through the wetland forest, the SCS's bulldozers had wrought a straight and shallow canal, its barren banks shorn of timber. Instead of letting the natural wetlands act as a sponge to prevent downstream flooding, the project simply hastened the floodwaters to downstream victims. The biologist who accompanied us explained that the project had destroyed the once-prolific perch and herring in the stream. The Maryland State Planning Department reported that the SCS's handiwork from 1942 to 1968 had destroyed almost half—11,960 of 23,717 acres—of the state's total wetlands loss. I calculated that twenty-four more projects like Gilbert Swamp would eliminate the last of Maryland's interior wetlands.

The channelization enthusiasts present explained that the newly dry wetlands would enable them to grow more tobacco and corn. I asked the SCS supervisor: "Is it good government to ban cigarette advertising on television, and at the same time bring more tobacco lands into production? Is it good government to pay farmers for *not* growing corn, and then pay for channelization so that farmers can grow *more* corn?" I didn't get an answer, but the SCS abandoned its channelization program in the early seventies.[1]

Our regional hearings were particularly effective. On the shores of Chesapeake Bay we identified the sources of the unchecked industrial, farm, and municipal pollution that were threatening the vast and beautiful "protein factory." In San Francisco we stopped the attempts of apartment builders and salt companies to fill in vital sections of that bay. In Miami we exposed those who were busy draining the Everglades to grow tomatoes that could be grown less expensively and better in the highlands of Mexico.

The effectiveness of our subcommittee was greatly enhanced by the presence of those three moderate Republicans. In the 1960s the House had about forty moderate Republicans—like John Lindsay of New York and John Anderson of Illinois. Their kind was all but eliminated by the Reagan revolution in the 1980s and the Gingrich revolution in the 1990s. This is a pity, for the golden age of good government (1948–1968) owed much to them. Great Britain under the Thatcher revolution made the same mistake, when fairminded Tories were weeded out and replaced by extremists.

THE REFUSE ACT OF 1899

The Conservation Subcommittee brought about the first real attack on water pollution in the nation's history. Early in 1970 Phineas Indritz, our dedicated staff director, found a federal statute that had been sleeping in the books for seventy years. The Refuse Act of 1899 provided that anyone who introduced a pollutant into any lake or stream, whether navigable or not, without obtaining a permit from the Army Corps of Engineers, had to pay a fine of $1,500 for each such discharge. Whoever reported such discharge to the proper authorities would be entitled to half the fine.

I decided to test this hoary statute. The Wisconsin Natural Resources Department had prepared a list of 270 firms, about equally divided between eastern and western Wisconsin, that were openly engaged in dumping wastes. The state had no enforcement powers, but it had requested—with no results—that companies voluntarily cease their pollution. So I prepared affidavits setting forth the exact details of each illegal discharge and filed them with the U.S. attorneys for eastern and western Wisconsin in April 1971. The attorney for the Western District shortly responded by bringing action under the Refuse Act against four major polluters. The court imposed fines on all and awarded me half. This, in accordance with a commitment I had made, I turned over to Wisconsin authorities to help pay the costs of building municipal sewage treatment plants, thus getting at another source of pollution.

Other prosecutions were shortly undertaken by blue-ribbon U.S. attorneys in other states. Whitney North Seymour in New York and Richard Thornburgh in Pennsylvania both successfully prosecuted industrial polluters under the Refuse Act.

On the basis of these successful prosecutions in Wisconsin, New York, and Pennsylvania, I prepared the Reuss Handy Kit, a guide for pollution watchers on how to use the Refuse Act. It included instructions on how to collect a sample of the discharge, how to write up the complaint and file it with the U.S. attorney, and how to monitor the proceedings. The kit was hugely popular, and several thousand were distributed and used around the country.

Not all U.S. attorneys were cooperative. The one in Milwaukee was not; he simply sat on the 131 complaints I sent him. A typical one he disregarded was my filing of March 20, 1970, against Moss-American, Inc., which for five years had been pouring creosote into the Little Menomonee River. On June 5, 1971, a neighborhood group attempted a cleanup campaign just downstream from the Moss plant. Nine people who waded in the stream were badly burned by the creosote pollution still clinging to the bottom, some so severely that they required hospitalization. This too failed to move the U.S. attorney from the Eastern District of Wisconsin.

Perhaps the most salutary effect of discovering the Refuse Act was that enforcing it soon convinced industry to stop fighting federal antipollution legislation and instead accept the reasonable federal regulatory system created by the Clean Water Act of 1972. Though much remains to be done, the nation has made great strides in cleaning up its waters.

ICE AGE RESERVE AND TRAIL

In 1958 I had a visit from an old friend, Milwaukee attorney-hiker-mountaineer Ray Zillmer. Ray was a salty soul, much given to Ben Franklin aphorisms; one I remember particularly was "When the bookkeeper starts talking overmuch of God, watch the Petty Cash!" Ray wanted to talk about his idea to set up a national park, to be called the Wisconsin Glacier National Forest Park, stretching for a thousand miles across the state from Sturgeon Bay to Interstate Park on the Minnesota border. The park would follow the moraines and other glacial land forms left by the receding Wisconsin glacier ten thousand years ago. It would tell the tale of how our land was formed and bring the joys of the outdoors to millions who lived nearby.

Later that year Ray led a group of enthusiasts over his projected park. We traveled from the old Wade House at Greenbush in the Northern Kettle Moraine State Forest to the St. Croix River in Polk County. Everyone along the route was enthusiastic and asked me to get the National Park Service (NPS) to do a study of the project's feasibility.

The NPS embarked on a lengthy study, which concluded that a thousand-mile national park would be too difficult to administer. It recommended instead a National Scientific Reserve of nine pearls along the route, to be jointly administered by the NPS and the state and to be hung on the string of a citizen-created Ice Age Trail. My bill to create the reserve became law on October 13, 1964. Sadly, Ray Zillmer had died four years earlier. The reserve's nine units, including Devil's Lake, the northern Kettle Moraine, Two Creeks Buried Forest, and Chippewa Moraine, were shortly established, many with interpretive centers.

Volunteers then began to lay out the trail, which I described in my 1980 guidebook, *On the Trail of the Ice Age*. On October 3, 1980, Congress designated it a National Scenic Trail, on a par with the Appalachian and Pacific Crest National Scenic Trails. The law directed that the trail follow the route outlined in my guidebook. I took pleasure over the years in hiking the trail with visitors from Washington, including Justice Douglas and Secretaries of the Interior Stewart Udall and Rogers Morton.

In 1996 I presented a "poem" at the dedication of ninety miles of newly opened Ice Age Trail in northwest Wisconsin's Indian Head country. Henry Wadsworth Longfellow must have turned in his grave.

> Near the shores of Gitche Gumee
> In the Indian Head dominion
> Ten thousand years ago the glacier
> Melted as the globe grew warm.
> (Gas-guzzlers, have a care, please,
> Lest global warming come again!)

Now the sons of Hiawatha
Saw this treasure at their doorstep,
Saw the need to keep it pristine,
Open just to fresh-faced hikers,
Babes in back-packs, nimble geezers.
In grand pow-wow the Ice Age zealots
Vowed to save the glacial land-forms,
Pledged to build a sylvan pathway
Through the ninety miles of forest.
And so on.

Nowhere is Wisconsin's Ice Age heritage more striking than in the Kettle Moraine forest of Washington and Waukesha Counties. In the 1930s Wisconsin began to acquire land for a Kettle Moraine State Forest that was to stretch for ninety miles over the moraines, drumlins (cigar-shaped mounds), eskers (long snakelike glacial remains), and kames (little glacial mountains) that the glacier had left. Unfortunately, after acquiring twenty-five miles at each end, money and willpower ran out; the most valuable portion, forty miles in the middle, remained largely unprotected and at the mercy of gravel quarries and developers. I was delighted when the Wisconsin Academy of Arts, Sciences and Letters decided in 1995 to undertake a study of the Kettle Moraine. Ody Fish, the academy's president, and I were asked to head up the task force. The study, completed in April 1996, presented a plan for a unique process of public-private cooperation.

Our report quoted Theodore Roosevelt—"a nation behaves well if the natural resources and assets which one generation turns over to the next are increased and not impaired in value"—and went on to say:

Because its soil is unsuitable for most farming, the Kettle Moraine remained much as it was when the first settlers saw it. In the 1930s, farsighted citizens of Wisconsin . . . created the Kettle Moraine State Forest, originally intended to span the entire 90 miles from north to south. . . .

The 40-mile stretch . . . is almost one-half privately owned, and therefore lacks both protection against destructive forestry, quarrying, and wetlands practices, and an integrated management policy. Sadly, . . . [it] contains some of the most notable geological and scenic features of all the Kettle Moraines. . . .

Today, legitimate but competing uses continue to convert portions of the unprotected Kettle Moraine in such a way as to interrupt its physical continuity on a piecemeal basis. These activities include logging as well as development of subdivisions, gravel pits, and highways. The task force agrees that, although such uses are not only inevitable but necessary, public recreation, environmental integrity, and aesthetics represent the highest and best use of essential portions of the Kettle Moraine.[2]

All told, the 1958–1972 era was a sparkling one for the environment. At the federal level were the clean air and clean water legislation, establishment of the Environmental Protection Agency and the Council of Environmental Advisers, expansion of the national park system, and passage of the Wilderness Act. In Wisconsin the contributions of two great conservationist governors, Gaylord Nelson and Warren Knowles, were equally epochal.

6

Full Employment
Without Inflation

It was natural that economics in general, and full employment without inflation in particular, should become an absorbing interest for me. Although I had not majored in economics in college, I had somewhat repaired that lack by self-study as a young lawyer in the mid-1930s. Bill Asmuth, a friend a few years my junior and a recent Harvard economics major, kindly undertook to be my economics tutor. On many a winter's night he imparted to me what he had learned.

In fact, the economist in our family is my wife, Margaret. She has a bachelor's degree in the "dismal science" from Bryn Mawr, a master's from the University of Chicago, and a doctoral degree from George Washington University. She went on to teach in the 1970s at George Washington and then at the new University of the District of Columbia, where she chaired the economics department.

My economics work-study program continued during my service with the Office of Price Administration, military government in Germany, and Marshall Plan. And it was not long before economics began to enter my life in Congress, if only in a minor way.

My committee assignments had been pallid, as befitted a first-termer from a Wisconsin then wholly without clout in the Democratic Congress. My major committee was Banking and Currency. Under the chairmanship of the aged Brent Spence, Democrat of Kentucky, the committee was a complete dud. He carried the committee rules, such as they were, in his head; new members like me were not allowed to ask questions, and our work product was negligible.

Somewhat more invigorating was Government Operations, my second committee. My first leader there was Bob Jones, an Alabama populist with a fine pack of coonhounds and a reverence for the Tennessee Valley Authority (TVA), which was supplying low-cost power to his district. Jones arranged a series of hearings by his Subcommittee on Public Works to rally support for the TVA. I attended faithfully and generally joined in the applause. But I felt I had to question whether the TVA should not pay the equivalent of a corporate income tax on its profits, so that a comparison of its rates with those of a private utility could be a fair one. This was of course anathema to Jones. We couldn't agree on a report, and none was made.

More fruitful were the subcommittee's hearings on the feasibility of the proposed St. Lawrence Seaway. The seaway, connecting Milwaukee with the Atlantic, was obviously of great importance to my district. Testimony at hearings throughout the Great Lakes was wildly favorable and gave the project forward momentum. But strangely, at a hearing I maneuvered for Milwaukee in 1957, where I expected the support to be the strongest, the civic leaders brought forward to boost the seaway dithered endlessly about whether it should be a publicly financed project or be left to private enterprise (i.e., forgotten about). The pusillanimous testimony of these star local witnesses so enraged my Michigan Democratic colleague Martha Griffith that she slipped me a note: "Dear Henry, as you know I've never thought too highly of you, but I have to say—you're too good for these people!" The seaway became law in 1958, with little thanks to our witnesses.

In 1957 a couple of events quickened my interest in economics. The first was recession. Essentially not one to rock the boat of post–New Deal prosperity but willing to take a little advice from his conservative cabinet, President Eisenhower mildly dampened spending and let the Federal Reserve mildly raise interest rates.[1] The result, not surprisingly, was that in 1958 the unemployment rate rose from 4.3 percent to 6.8 percent, followed by a Democratic victory in the 1958 congressional elections. Clearly, government made a difference in whether an American could get or keep a job.

The second event was that in mid-1958 a vacancy came up on the Joint Economic Committee, for which I had been applying from my first day in Congress. The leitmotif of the Joint Economic Committee was set forth in the epochal Employment Act of 1946. The act boldly declared that "it is the continuing policy and responsibility of the Federal Government to promote maximum employment, production, and purchasing power"—briefly, full employment without inflation. Congress had then created the Joint Economic Committee to hold periodic hearings on how well the government was meeting this mandate and to issue reports on what additional policies might be needed. Obviously, the JEC was where the action would be, and I wanted on.

Appointments in the House of Representatives to the Joint Economic Committee are the exclusive privilege of the Speaker when the Democrats hold the majority, as opposed to all the rest of the committee assignments, which are disbursed by other party leaders. And the Speaker was still Sam Rayburn of Texas, whom I had offended a few days before with my speech on the House floor opposing Eisenhower's dispatch of U.S. troops to Lebanon. Would the Speaker take out his wrath on the rebellious sophomore from Wisconsin who had undercut our troops then on foreign soil? Fortunately for me, Mr. Sam was a big man, without rancor even against someone who had recently outraged him. He appointed me. I served on the JEC for a quarter-century and ended up as its chair, fighting a losing battle against Reaganomics in 1981–1982.

A CONFLICT?

Safely installed on the JEC, I immediately had to confront the looming new question: whether full employment without inflation is a contradiction in terms. If we really achieved full employment—say, the 3 percent level of prosperous 1951–1953—wouldn't that simply bring about demand inflation (too much money would be chasing too few goods)? Conversely, if we pulled inflation down to where prices were stable, wouldn't the slackened activity simply bring about higher unemployment? The obvious conflict between the two goals was troublesome.

I had seen at firsthand the baneful effects of both unemployment and inflation. During the depression years of 1939 and 1940, when I was an assistant Milwaukee County corporation counsel, I had witnessed how mass joblessness had come close to breaking up our society.

Earlier I had had a chance to see the opposite specter, inflation, at its most hideous. In 1923 I had accompanied my father on a walking tour of the Black Forest in Germany, so as an eleven year old I saw what skyrocketing inflation could do to the lives of ordinary people. A lunch in a country inn, which cost a million marks when you ordered, could be tripled by the time you paid the bill. With the German currency hopelessly inflated, municipalities were forced to issue Notgeld (emergency money), beautifully engraved but soon worthless. I assembled a boy's collection of 1923 Notgeld (now in the Milwaukee Public Library).

Thus in 1957 I was full of enthusiasm to fight both unemployment and inflation. For starters, the fight was to be carried on in the good old macroeconomic Keynesian way by maintaining aggregate spending power in the economy, private and public, through fiscal policies (appropriations and taxes) and monetary policies (interest rates). One hoped that Keynes-in-America would prove just right to keep unemployment low without causing inflation. Modest deficits need not be worrisome, provided that the ability to run large ones was retained as a weapon if depression should threaten again.

Attention to macroeconomics meant above all concern that the federal budget, and its levels of spending and taxing, stimulated the economy toward full employment and restrained it from inflation.

So budgetary decisions began to appear strongly on my agenda. I tried to follow the sage advice of Sen. Paul Douglas: "A liberal does not have to be a spendthrift." During the cold war I found what I viewed as swollen military spending to be a recurring target for sensible limitation. Another target was subsidies for the supersonic transport plane, which we finally ended, thus avoiding the Franco-British Concorde fiasco. Still another was subsidies to large corporate farms for idling land. I succeeded in attaching an amendment to the 1958 agricultural appropriations bill that limited annual subsidy payments to any one farm to $3,000. This confined the federal largess to the family-sized farmer who really needed it. But shortly thereafter Eisenhower's secretary of agriculture, Ezra Taft Benson, found a sneaky way around my amendment—divide a huge corporate farm into hundreds of little separate farms and give each one a check for $3,000.

As with expenditures, so with taxation. This too became a new imperative for me. My qualification here was an exemplary tax course I had taken at Harvard Law from Dean Erwin Griswold, plus on-the-job training over the years preparing my own income tax returns. If we have an appalling income tax structure today, it is largely because powerful Ways and Means Committee chairmen for years allowed each committee member, Democrat or Republican, to add a little special-interest loophole to that year's omnibus tax bill as it was wending its way through the committee. The result was frightful to behold.

Attacking these special-interest tax loopholes was a difficult business, because arousing the public's attention was hard. My only success, in 1971, was in eliminating the "flower bond" loophole, which permitted wealthy taxpayers to buy special treasury bonds at a discount—say, at $85 for a $100 bond—and turn them in to the treasury upon the taxpayer's death for a $100-a-bond credit on the estate tax, thus netting a nice windfall of $15 per bond.

I decided that a more fundamental approach was needed, one that would shame the Ways and Means Committee into ending its disgusting habit of accepting campaign contributions, creating tax loopholes for the contributors, who thus had more money and could make larger campaign contributions, and so on and on and on. I appeared before Ways and Means in 1972 to testify from an elaborate exhibit I had had constructed, which I called my Flow Chart. It depicted graphically the flow of contributions to committee members, the new tax loopholes they created, and the round-trip back to the committee members from the contributors of the loot from the loopholes. The committee was not amused, particularly the ranking Republican, John Byrnes of Wisconsin, who had recently been discovered arranging a tax favor for a mortgage company that had sold him its stock on a preferential basis.

I soon realized that my exclusively *macroeconomic* approach—one concerned simply with aggregate fiscal and monetary policies—might be what was causing the incompatibility between the two goals of maximum employment and minimum inflation. Perhaps there were *microeconomic* approaches, ones that committed the venial sin of interfering with the free market, that might let us get closer to both goals.

Looking first at the employment side, I kept plugging for a program of public jobs, in addition to those that could be created by a market economy. In 1964 my first book, *The Critical Decade,* addressed the need for a federal "work-and-learn" program:

The immediate problem of the unemployed is that they need jobs, and they need them now.

I have suggested a "work-and-learn" program under which Federal grants would be made to local communities or nonprofit institutions such as hospitals for worthwhile local projects. . . . The job would consist partly in work on a project, partly in going to school—either job training at a vocational school, or learning to read and write at a continuation school. Thus the program would come to grips with our grave social problems of disillusion and discrimination by providing self-respect through immediate work, and a new skill, even if it be only the gift of literacy, for the future. In the relatively rare case of someone needing no training, there could be just the job. . . .

The local community or nonprofit institution would be required to do its part. It would have to meet the non-labor costs, and to supply supervision. Projects would be those with a high labor intensity, such as modifying the land for a new recreation area near a metropolitan center, or helping in a neighborhood or downtown "clean-up" campaign. In order to receive support, the project would have to be established as additional to anything that would be undertaken without the work-and-learn program.[2]

Programs like "work and learn" were soon to be provided under Lyndon Johnson's War on Poverty. They succeeded in nudging unemployment lower than what could have been achieved by relying on macroeconomic stimulus alone. Unfortunately, the War on Poverty expired before it really had a chance to achieve its goal. It was undermined by diversions of its appropriations to pay for the runaway costs of the Vietnam War and by the public's loss of confidence in its government.

Today, thirty years later, I believe the same need exists for public employment programs to supplement the jobs the market creates.

I am pleased that Wisconsin today is testing a "work-and-learn" approach to finding jobs for those forced off welfare. Republican governor Tommy Thompson early on vowed to end "welfare as we know it" but did nothing to provide jobs for those about to become welfare graduates. His

Democratic opponents, mainly in the larger cities, at first were content to defend the income-maintenance welfare programs in place since the 1930s. But more recently the old Wisconsin Idea of pioneering new approaches to old problems has taken hold. The Republican governor and the Democratic legislature both supported Wisconsin Works, a program to offer jobs, private and public, supplemented by training, child care, and health insurance, as the alternative to welfare.

It is too early to tell whether Wisconsin Works will prove to be successful welfare reform. But the creative tension brought about by Republicans' and Democrats' trying to blend their historic principles to solve a major problem gives at least some hope.

Nationally, we need something like the War on Poverty's public service programs to provide jobs for those whom the market economy fails.

Someone who advocates public service jobs today must offer a way of paying for them that does not increase the national deficit. I have proposed just that.[3]

Everyone agrees that the nation's infrastructure needs repair. Pockmarked streets and roads, collapsing bridges, overcrowded airports, unsafe railroads, nonexistent mass transit, corrupted water supplies, inadequate waste disposal—all mock us daily and cost us dearly. A reasonable infrastructure program could create about 120,000 additional construction jobs a year.

How could we fund an infrastructure program that does not increase budget deficits? For starters, we could look at the revenue lost through the home-equity income tax deduction, which allows home owners to deduct the interest they pay on bank loans of up to $100,000 and permits them to use the money for all sorts of purposes. The deduction costs the treasury at least $3 billion a year, and the benefits go mainly to the top 20 percent of American households. Apart from the obvious inequity, why, when pundits are calling for more investment and less consumer spending, should we continue to subsidize consumption?

The banks that have sponsored and prospered from the home-equity deduction would resist its reduction or elimination. Nevertheless, eliminating it would permit a deficit-neutral shift from consumption to investment in jobs-producing infrastructure work.

Another excellent candidate for deficit-neutral budget restructuring is low-income housing. The Department of Housing and Urban Development has estimated a current need for at least four million low-income housing units. Annual production, almost all the result of the Low Income Housing Tax Credit, is about 200,000 units. That is barely enough to keep up with the annual increase in need for affordable low-income housing. Why not triple the production level for new and rehabilitated housing by expanding the credit? At this rate, it would take about seven years to accomplish the goal set by the late senator Robert Taft in his Housing Act of 1949 — a decent home in a livable environment for every American.

Needless to say, getting serious about affordable housing must be a part of any effort to combat poverty and crime. The areas of greatest need for building or rehabilitating low-income housing closely track the areas of our worst urban and rural unemployment. Programs designed to transform such areas — those for controlling crime, drugs, and family disintegration; improving health and education; and encouraging neighborhood cooperation — cannot succeed unless jobs and homes are important components. Equally, welfare reforms that cut recipients from the rolls after two years cannot work unless jobs are waiting for "graduates" of the welfare system.

But where is the funding for an expanded Low Income Housing Tax Credit to come from? Examination of the federal tax subsidies for housing shows that $1.5 billion annually goes to the credit and $45 billion goes to the mortgage interest deduction for home owners. This deduction enables home owners to deduct the interest on mortgages as high as $1 million. At the current mortgage rate of about 7.5 percent, that means an annual deduction of $75,000, or reduction in tax of more than $30,000 for high-bracket taxpayers every year for the life of a thirty-year mortgage.

The deduction is inequitable, because it benefits mainly the top 20 percent of U.S. taxpayers, enabling them to increase their consumption and savings. It also misallocates investment, toward private mansions and away from productive plant and equipment.

Still another harmful effect of the home-mortgage interest deduction is that it leads to urban sprawl. Subsidizing the building of extralarge homes on extralarge lots an extralong distance from town gobbles up precious green space, makes mass transit so costly as not to be feasible, and saddles taxpayers with the cost of unnecessary new roads, sewer and water facilities, and utilities. And it erects enclaves of large homes whose owners often resist the building nearby of affordable smaller homes for the police officers and fire fighters who serve them.

Lowering the $1 million ceiling to the first $300,000 of a mortgage, or limiting the amount of the deduction on mortgage interest to $20,000 on a joint return, would add more than $3 billion annually to treasury revenues, which we could then channel into an expanded Low Income Housing Tax Credit that would triple current production and create about 400,000 new jobs in building and rehabilitating homes.

From the standpoint of jobs, trading reductions in the home-equity and home-mortgage tax preferences for increases in infrastructure and housing would be advantageous. A dollar spent on workers and materials to fill potholes, repair sewers, or build low-income housing would create jobs directly, without appreciable leakage. The dollar obtained by cutting back on the tax preferences would come from upper-income taxpayers who likely would have spent at least part of their tax break for foreign-made goods and for investments outside the United States that create no jobs here.

Of course, the lobbies for the banking and real estate industries will fight any attempt to cut the home-equity and home mortgage–interest deductions, asserting that it will deal a blow to home ownership. Moreover, even with diminished mortgage-interest deductions, home owners would still enjoy their deduction for state and local property taxes on owner-occupied homes ($14 billion annually in lost revenues) and their virtual avoidance of capital gains on home sales (another $20 billion annually).

The combined job-creating effect of refocusing on infrastructure and housing—without affecting the national deficit—could be as many as 520,000 new construction jobs, plus an additional 400,000 to 600,000 jobs throughout the economy as spending by the new holders of those construction jobs begins to percolate upward.

An incidental benefit of this refocusing would be to provide a better way of fighting incipient inflation than tightening money and raising interest rates generally, as the Federal Reserve has done before and may do again. Such a monetary "preemptive strike" by the Fed, though ostensibly aimed at excessive borrowing for consumption and at the "irrational exuberance" of the stock market—is just what the nation doesn't need. Reducing the home-equity and the home-mortgage interest deductions, on the other hand, would directly curtail consumption without materially affecting productive investment. The executive branch, Congress, and the Fed act as if they live in different worlds; instead, they should get together on what is surely the least costly first step in slaying the specter of inflation: plugging the tax loopholes that cause inflation. Raising interest rates should be a last resort in the fight against inflation, not the first.

THE WAGE-PRICE SPIRAL

On the inflation-fighting side, as on the jobs side, I looked for microeconomic methods that would supplement macroeconomic budgetary and monetary policies. Something new appeared in the late 1950s—administered price inflation, caused by the interaction of powerful unions and powerful industries like steel and autos. The Federal Reserve had tried to combat this spiral of wage-price inflation with tight money in 1955–1957. This did nothing to cure the wage-price spiral; it simply brought on a recession.

In 1959 Sen. Joe Clark, Democrat of Pennsylvania, and I introduced legislation that would have required public hearings on proposed wage and price increases in major industries, in order "to bring to bear an informed public opinion on wage and price increases which in [the president's] judgment appear to threaten national economic stability."

A powerful array of forces lined up against the Clark-Reuss proposal. The Eisenhower administration threatened a veto because the bill "would tend to substitute government inquiry into the reasons for, and the justifiability of, any price increase for our traditional ideals of prices set in response to free-market forces." The National Association of Manufacturers said the bill would "generally retard technological improvements and the forward progress of our economy." The U.S. Chamber of Commerce opposed it as signaling "the end of consumer sovereignty and freedom." U.S. Steel chairman Roger M. Blough said it would lead to "gradual destruction of the greatest industrial machine the world has ever known."

Labor was equally opposed. The AFL-CIO proclaimed that the bill "served no useful purpose." David J. McDonald, president of the United Steelworkers, called it a "radical departure from the national policy of free collective bargaining."

A House Government Operations subcommittee, evidently feeling that the contentions of Big Business and Big Labor canceled each other out, favorably reported our bill. But with a veto threatened, the bill died there.

The orderly procedures of the Clark-Reuss bill were certainly preferable to what actually happened. In April 1962, shortly after the United Steelworkers union settled for a moderate wage increase from the U.S. Steel Corporation, Big Steel suddenly announced a sharp increase in steel prices. President Kennedy's temper flared: he denounced the corporation's leaders as "sons-of-bitches" and threatened antitrust suits and IRS audits. Fortunately, Big Steel backed down and withdrew its price increase.

There followed, under the guidance of Walter W. Heller, chief of the Council of Economic Advisers (CEA) and a fellow Milwaukeean who had made a great reputation with his fiscal studies, a regime of wage-price guideposts that served well as a microeconomic supplement to the administration's overall Keynesian macroeconomic stance. Heller was ably flanked by his two CEA colleagues, Kermit Gordon and James Tobin.

Thus by the mid-1960s the nation was enjoying the best of both worlds —strong growth in jobs and production by macroeconomic methods, supplemented on the job side by microeconomic jobs programs and on the inflation side by microeconomic wage-price guideposts.

This was the golden age of full employment without inflation—neither inflation nor deflation, as some wit said, but just plain "flation." More, this was attained with a low and manageable national debt. We have never equaled it since. As I write, we have a booming national economy, with inflation held down not by wage-price guideposts but by global competition and the progressive weakening of labor unions; no War on Poverty; and recent cuts in capital gains and estate taxes that increase the national debt at one of the better times in history to lower it.

AFTER THE GOLDEN AGE

After the mid-1960s economics became bleak. Vietnam stalled LBJ's War on Poverty. Richard Nixon, proclaiming himself a born-again Keynesian, was all stimulus—continuing the war in Vietnam and encouraging George Romney, secretary of housing and urban development, in the largest publicly assisted housing program yet and Federal Reserve Board chairman Arthur Burns to keep interest rates low. (Chapter 7 describes Nixon's sensible closing of the gold window in 1971, and his simultaneous less sensible imposition of wage-price controls to fight a modest 4 percent inflation.)

With the enormous oil price increases of the Organization of Petroleum Exporting Countries—it quadrupled them in 1973 and doubled them in 1978—stagflation took over. The price increases in oil acted as a huge tax, taking out of the economy purchasing power needed to sustain growth. They also percolated throughout the system and caused a general price spiral. Nixon's successor, Gerald R. Ford, whom I had liked and respected as a House member from Michigan, was never able to figure out whether stagnation or inflation was the problem while he was president. In fact, it was both, and Ford's Whip Inflation Now buttons appeared just in time to confront the recession.

On taking office in 1977, Jimmy Carter immediately declared our oil crisis the "moral equivalent of war." A special committee in the House— the Ad Hoc Energy Committee—was convened to develop a comprehensive program to deal with the problem, and I was one of the multitude who served on it. After months of wrangling it produced a voluminous program containing everything but the one element that could have made sense. That would have been authority to ration gasoline to its more essential uses and thus to quiet the demand that was sending gas prices skyrocketing. This would have put some restraint on the devastating general inflation that gasoline and oil prices were causing.

I prepared a gasoline rationing program, based on successful exercises in World War II and the Korean War. Briefly, auto owners would have been assured of enough gas coupons to commute to work, shop, and attend to other essentials; pleasure driving would have to be limited. But neither the administration nor the Ad Hoc Energy Committee was willing to buy my proposal. Price controls and rationing were in disfavor after Nixon's illfated 1971 experiment.

With nothing to restrain OPEC's oil price increases, inflation became endemic. To keep the economy going, the Federal Reserve hesitated to raise interest rates. The resulting increases in the money supply fueled savage increases in the prices of land, homes, and collectibles. As the situation spun out of control, a new Federal Reserve chairman, Paul Volcker, was brought on in October 1979. He promptly cranked interest rates up to an unprecedented level of 20 percent or more in the waning days of the Carter administration and the early days of Ronald Reagan's, thus precipitating a recession and mass unemployment. An ill-advised Carter became the first Democratic president since Thomas Jefferson and his embargo on exports to create a recession. Carter has brilliantly atoned for his mediocre presidency by establishing himself as the best ex-president since Jefferson, with splendid contributions to everything from low-income housing to world peace.

Reagan's first two years, 1981–1982, were my last two in Washington. Aware that his new economic program would need some rebuttal, I gave up my banking committee chairmanship and took over that of the Joint Economic Committee. The JEC had fallen upon lackluster days during the Carter administration, inordinately preoccupied with recommending tax cuts for the wealthy, a proposal that not surprisingly produced JEC reports championed by both parties (with a few dissents from me and others).

The first JEC report under my chairmanship, that of March 1981, was highly critical of Reagan's program, on the obvious ground that huge tax cuts for the wealthy, combined with large increases in military spending, would produce huge deficits, with consequent impairment of the nation's ability to conduct its affairs. The Republicans, naturally, refused to join in the committee report and produced their own report proclaiming that all was right with Reaganomics. At the press conference held to announce our reports, the Republicans wept over the Democrats' "breach of bipartisanship." And the press reported this sad fact—that Republicans and Democrats disagreed!—as the main news. So the media failed to fully report this first reasoned critique of Reaganomics.

The triumph of Reaganomics occurred on July 4, 1981, when the House, with a majority of Democrats joining in, passed the Reagan Tax Act. I called it a "radical redistribution of income in this country from moderate-income people to the top 10 percent." And I could not forgive my party's betrayal of its principles: "I am sad about today's vote—and for the future of my country, and the future of my party, the Democrats."

One Democrat who did not run for cover was Speaker Tip O'Neill. Describing Reagan as "Herbert Hoover with a smile," O'Neill fought Reaganomics with all his considerable might. History will deal kindly with Tip, a Speaker with a soul.

By the summer of 1982 the country was in a deep recession, and Reaganomics was in full retreat. Murray Wiedenbaum, Reagan's chief economic adviser, testified before the JEC on the events of 1981 and asserted that the Reagan administration had known all along that its plan could precipitate a huge deficit and that it was thus not surprised when this turned out to be the case. "Where is all this awareness written down?" I asked, for the official administration documents in early 1981 had all denied a deficit would result, claiming instead that the magic of Reaganomics would bring such prosperity to the land that the deficit would disappear. "Why, it's all set forth in our internal plan of February 1981," replied Wiedenbaum. I demanded to see the document; Wiedenbaum refused, citing executive privilege. I replied that he had stepped down from his executive pedestal by bragging about the document and that he had to produce it immediately. The dispute dragged on to the end of the year. Ten years later the JEC staff found it had had the document in its files all along and that the document did indeed disclose the great GOP secret—that Reaganomics would swell the deficit. Shortly after this discovery I ran into Murray while gazing at the impressionists at the Metropolitan Museum of Art in New York and amiably told him of our startling find.

My last House speech, at the end of 1982, borrowed from the Book of Common Prayer: "We have done many things we ought not to have done. We have left undone many things we ought to have done. And there is no health in us." As I retired from Congress in January 1983, I gave my views on Reaganomics to editor Tyler Bridges in *People and Taxes*:

P&T: The supply siders compare the 1981 Reagan tax cut with the 1964 Kennedy-Johnson tax cut, which helped stimulate economic growth. Is this a valid comparison?

REUSS: No, it's not. There are several important differences between the Kennedy-Johnson 1964 tax cut and the Reagan tax cut of 1981. One important difference was that the 1964 tax cut was achieved at a time of almost zero inflation. . . .

A second difference was that the Reagan tax cut was badly slanted and skewed toward people at the top of the income scale. They got not only the benefits of a percentage tax cut . . . but they also got special niceties such as the immediate reduction of the top bracket from 70 to 50 percent, the immediate reduction of the capital gains bracket from 28 to 20 percent, huge and quite prompt reductions in corporate taxes and in estate and gift taxes, all of which were radically different from the Kennedy-Johnson 1964 tax cut. So the analogy simply does not hold.

P&T: Over the years, Congress has been giving more and more tax breaks to business in the name of increasing investment and increasing productivity. Yet, while Congress has been giving business these tax breaks, investments have actually been going down, the economy has been getting worse, productivity has been going down. It seems that tax breaks don't do anything at all to help the economy.

REUSS: You are right. Most of these business incentives are so badly or so deceptively crafted that instead of really representing a rifle-shot subsidy for actual investment, they just represent a bonanza or giveaway to a corporate interest that in many cases isn't used for capital investment at all. . . .

P&T: . . . Why have corporations been getting more and more tax breaks over the years?

REUSS: I think my Flow Chart of ten years ago illustrates it. It's the golden rule: Those who have the gold make the rules. . . .

Less is raised by the corporate income tax, estate and gift taxes, the income tax, and hence one of several things has to happen. Either essential programs are short-changed and that [has happened] to a degree, or reliance is placed on more regressive taxes that state and local governments in their agony turn to, such as higher sales and property taxes specifically. Or the deficit gets bigger and bigger. All of those phenomena are now in full course.

P&T: Is there a direct relationship between the outcome of tax legislation and campaign contributions to Congressmen?

REUSS: As my 1972 Flow Chart indicated, I think it is a very considerable nexus. I suspect that campaign contributors don't always make a contribution for love. . . .

P&T: . . . Could we move towards a simplified tax system with few or no deductions?

REUSS: We certainly should. And if we did that, that would permit a still progressive but lower bracket for all taxpayers. It isn't going to happen, though, if the matter is left to Congress. Congress, by its very nature, is a set of 535 baronies, and it is subject to being picked off in detail.

What we need is a forceful presidential voice who can rally public opinion. I know public opinion is ready to be rallied on this, because the 80 percent of Americans who lie between the very poor and the very rich are up in arms and ready to join a taxpayer's revolt because the burden is being shifted onto them. . . . . .

We Democrats are adrift, and we should heed the advice of our great leader Franklin Delano Roosevelt. After the Democrats' victory in the 1936 election—a comparable or even greater victory than the one we scored in 1982—FDR spoke to a Democratic victory gathering at the Mayflower Hotel in Washington in early 1937. FDR said to his fellow Democrats: "If we don't have the courage to lead the American people where they want to go, who will?"

. . . However, it is sometimes given to a political party to have a second chance, and we Democrats now have it. But if we go the way of "know-nothingism" and "me-tooism," the nation will soon decide that it wants Republicans. The people know where the Republicans are and how to vote them in. So I close with the hope that FDR's rhetorical question will be heeded.[4]

7

International Economics

MONEY

Until the mid-1960s the country's major economic preoccupation was domestic full employment without inflation. As Chapter 6 describes, this was achieved by a macroeconomic practice of ensuring adequate demand by mildly stimulative tax, spending, and interest-rate policies, supported by microeconomic measures of wage-price guideposts to combat cost-push inflation, and the War on Poverty to combat structural unemployment and open job opportunities to the poor and underemployed.[1]

Now something new appeared. For the first time our Joint Economic Committee hearings exposed me to the international forces—gold, currency exchanges, the balance of payments—that were beginning to affect our domestic economic policies.

Until the start of World War I in 1914, the United States, Britain, and most of the industrialized countries were on the so-called gold standard. War spending necessitated its temporary abandonment.

For the United States the gold standard meant that the dollar was convertible into gold at $20.67 an ounce. This was supposed to limit inflation by restricting the creation of new money to the amount of gold presented to the treasury for conversion into dollars. In practice, the gold standard worked only erratically. When new gold was discovered in Alaska or South Africa, the sudden increase in money caused inflation. When new discovery lagged, not enough new currency was in circulation, and panic and depression ensued.

Nonetheless, the United States returned to the gold standard in the 1920s. Because it helped lead to the Great Depression, FDR abandoned the gold standard in 1934. As World War II neared its end, the victorious nations wanted an international monetary system that combined some stability of exchange rates with a degree of domestic control over interest rates and the money supply by the participating countries. At Bretton Woods in New Hampshire in 1944, they established a system of "fixed but adjustable exchange rates." Participating countries were to peg their exchange rates to the dollar, which the United States, with its vast gold reserves, agreed to convert into gold at $35 an ounce.

Following Bretton Woods, the United States generously embarked on a campaign to enable the impoverished countries of Europe and Japan to revive their economies. The United States sharply reduced its tariffs so that trading partners might increase their exports. Their currencies were initially set at low levels against the dollar for the same purpose. The strategy worked so well that our trading partners steadily acquired ever-larger stocks of dollars in their reserves. As the 1960s progressed, it became apparent that U.S. gold reserves would not be adequate to meet forever our obligation under the Bretton Woods "gold exchange standard" to supply gold for dollars presented to the U.S. Treasury.

I recognized that this was an incipient crisis that was getting no congressional attention. I asked for, and in 1965 was granted, a new subcommittee to focus on the problem, the Subcommittee on International Exchange and Payments. We began a series of in-depth studies and hearings. Once again I was lucky to have an admirable opposite number in Rep. Bob Ellsworth of Kansas, the ranking Republican.

Not surprisingly, our subcommittee was well supplied with witnesses to advise on how to respond to the oncoming crisis. The gold lobby, made up of mining companies, dealers in bullion, writers of gold newsletters, and assorted true believers, strongly advocated a return to the classic gold standard. Their spiritual leader was President Charles de Gaulle of France, who advocated going back to the gold standard as it existed before World War I.

Because hardly anyone could follow the reasoning behind this crusade for the gold standard — or against it, for that matter — I decided that a little spoof might be in order. Speaking from the House floor on March 21, 1968, I said:

Mr. Speaker, President de Gaulle has just handed a blow to the monetary authorities of the free world. He favors a pure gold standard because of its "immutability, impartiality, and universality."

As a friend of France, I share the General's concern at the present fragmentary role of gold.

I differ from him only in that he does not go far enough. The price of gold has wavered on the Paris Bourse in the last week between $44 and $37.

Surely we can find a monetary medium more immutable than gold.

I call the attention of the French monetary authorities to the existence of a medium which fits these specifications, and has an historic background at once historic and wholly French.

I refer, of course, to beaver pelts. During the period of France's sovereignty over what is now the Great State of Wisconsin, from 1634 to 1763, the beaver pelt was the universal medium of exchange. Immutable, impartial, and universal, it governed transactions in all commodities. A beaver pelt purchased two pounds of sugar, twenty fish hooks, or a fine linen handkerchief. . . .

The beaver, for his part, provided an unfailing expanding currency. Each beaver married couple, as the French naturalist Buffon has observed, produced a litter of exactly four beaver kits every spring.

This orderly beaver population increase has continued. According to the last census, Wisconsin today boasts some seventy thousand beavers. At $10 a pelt, we can continue to furnish a steady supply to the monetary world.

How comforting, Mr. Speaker, to rely on a monetary supply under the control of friendly Wisconsin, rather than on a metal like gold which is subject to the control of its two major producers, the Soviet Union and South Africa.

As France took the lead in making the beaver pelt legal tender three hundred years ago, surely it can do so today.

I should report that many Wisconsin trappers feel that the present price of $10 a beaver pelt is too low. If President de Gaulle should feel it necessary that the new basic medium should be doubled in price in order to provide sufficient liquidity, Wisconsin will not want to stand in the way.

A second player, the U.S. Treasury, favored direct controls over U.S. investment abroad as the way to diminish the supply of dollars in foreign hands. This proved difficult to enforce and of doubtful effectiveness.

A third group, made up of respected monetary economists of primarily European origin—Robert Triffin of Belgium, Fritz Machlup of Hungary, Gottfried Haberler and William Fellner of Austria, and others—favored us with more original recommendations. Some, like Triffin, advocated establishing a new international monetary unit. Others, like Machlup, saw no great harm in abandoning the Bretton Woods "fixed but adjustable exchange rate" regime in favor of freely floating exchange rates.

These practitioners of the art of international money had become known as the Bellagio group, from the enchanting villa on Lake Como in Italy that was their central meeting place. I soon became a member of the group and profited much not only from their discussions but from their choices of meeting places, such as Taormina in Sicily, Estoril in Portugal, and Málaga in Spain.

By 1970 the crisis of our wide-open gold window came closer. The Vietnam War had added greatly to the supply of dollars in the reserves of other countries. The United States obviously could not forever wiggle out of its commitment to supply gold for the dollars our creditor countries might choose to present at the treasury's gold window. Meanwhile, we were being disingenuous with our friends by urging them not to convert their dollars into gold. If the dollar were ever to be devalued by a closing of the gold window, they would stand to lose heavily for their friendly cooperation.

In vain I sought to convince the Nixon administration that the sooner it closed the gold window and let the dollar find its proper level, the better. John Connally, secretary of the treasury, assured me at a meeting in his office that the administration would never close the gold window and a few days later said so publicly. The only course left to me, I decided, was to go public with my belief that the emperor had no clothes. On August 6, 1971, my subcommittee issued a report recommending that the gold window be closed, the dollar be allowed to find a more realistic level, and a new post–Bretton Woods regime be inaugurated.

A few days later, on August 15, with Congress adjourned for the August recess, I was in Vienna preparing for a journey to eastern Europe. Awakened at dawn by the Associated Press, I was told of the action President Nixon had just taken—he had closed the gold window, imposed a 10 percent surcharge on all our imports, and established across-the-board wage-and-price controls. I applauded the closing of the window, opposed the protectionist import surcharge, and had my doubts of the need for wage-price controls with inflation running at a relatively modest 4 percent.

Of course, our August 6 report had forced the administration to close the gold window. At the treasury's request friendly countries had been holding back on demanding gold for dollars. After our report they started telling the treasury that they could no longer risk huge exchange losses. So action was the treasury's only choice. The longer the administration waited, the worse the betrayal of friendly countries would be.

Nixon's 10 percent surcharge on imports did not last long. Its effect on our trading partners, particularly Canada, was disastrous, and it was withdrawn within weeks.

As for the wage-price controls, their short-term effect was salubrious, both for the economy and for Nixon's reelection. With the controls keeping inflation down, and with an easy money policy stimulating the economy, Nixon could point to low unemployment and low inflation. This helped Nixon in his forty-nine-state landslide victory over George McGovern in November 1972. Thereafter the controls were administered in a halfhearted manner and were finally removed in 1974 just when inflation was starting to gallop.

Gold was not quite dead after the closing of the gold window in August 1971. The gold lobby still longed for a restoration of some monetary role, domestic or foreign, for the precious metal. One of the Reagan administration's first acts in 1981 was to set up the Gold Commission to determine whether such a role could be found. I asked the Speaker to appoint me to the commission and watched attentively, lest the gold bugs on the commission find such a role. In the end, the commission could find none. Gold as money appears no longer to be an issue.

One idea heavily debated in the Bellagio group does seem to have a future. An international monetary unit such as Bob Triffin advocated may actually be in the offing for members of the European Union. As I write, the euro is scheduled to appear officially in 1999. I think the introduction of the euro will require the European Union to strengthen the role of the European Parliament in regard to the new European central bank in order to introduce an element of democratic control over the technocratic monetary authorities. It will also require coordinated fiscal policies.

If the euro repairs its deficiencies, and if it works, it may be time for Canada and the United States, already joined for trade purposes in the North American Free Trade Agreement, to consider coordinating their fiscal policies and then set up a single U.S.-Canadian dollar. The gains in trade, investment, and tourism would seem to be considerable and the risks manageable. If the time for such consideration arrives, the minutes of the Bellagio group would be helpful.

TRADE

I believed in free trade when I came to Congress, and I never budged from that belief. It brings real benefits to consumers and to the vast majority of workers and businesses. Assistance can and should be provided to those workers and businesses adversely affected by imports. The first bill I introduced in Congress was to provide such aid, and the principle has been incorporated in our trade legislation over the years.

My espousal of free trade has sometimes led me into conflict with my most faithful supporters, the labor unions. In the 1970s the United Steelworkers promoted the Burke-Hartke bill, which would have imposed rigid quotas on imported steel. The Milwaukee Steelworkers unions, disappointed that I had failed to sign on as cosponsor of Burke-Hartke, asked me to explain my stand. After reciting my long history of standing shoulder to shoulder with the Steelworkers, I got to the point: "Look, we in Wisconsin don't *make* steel; we *use* steel, and the lower the cost of our raw material, the more secure our jobs." I was allowed to depart in peace.

A few years later an equally friendly union, the United Auto Workers, asked my support for its "local content" legislation, which would have required imported automobiles to have a high percentage of American-made parts. Here again the proposal had its appeal, but it would have been a major departure from free trade that would have led to retaliation from our trading partners. So I said no but sadly, because in my audience were many men and women who at election time had stood by me at the plant gates in the rain.

Too much free trade can be a bad thing if it results in drawing down our supply of a particular commodity without sufficient warning. This is exactly what happened in the early 1970s when a Soviet crop failure brought about demands for huge imports of American wheat, causing turmoil in world markets.

I accompanied Sen. Hubert Humphrey on a 1976 JEC trip to the Soviet

Union and Poland to determine whether we could have had better notice of the Soviet crop failure. We found the cause: a single U.S. agricultural attaché in the American embassy in Moscow was supposed to do all the crop forecasting for the entire Soviet Union. This was one case where more, rather than fewer, U.S. personnel would have been in order. We so recommended on our return, and the U.S. agricultural staff was beefed up.[2]

Import substitution is the term used to describe a country's setting up its own industry to replace goods it previously imported from another country. If undertaken behind a protective tariff, this is a bad idea (except for a developing country, and then only for a transitional period), because it misallocates resources. But import substitution is no sin when it produces goods that do not enjoy a protective tariff. I became involved in a couple of import substitutions of this unsinful nature.

The 1970s saw the demise of many of Wisconsin's mom-and-pop country crossroads factories that made those delicious smelly soft cheeses. They were done in by the supermarkets, which were concentrating on cardboard cheese with a long shelf life. Meanwhile, a new generation of upwardly mobile young professionals was gorging itself on runny Brie and Camembert imported from Normandy. I asked myself: why not produce these soft cheeses in Wisconsin, using milk from Wisconsin cows and know-how from unemployed Wisconsin cheese makers? I approached the firm of Besnier et Fils, premiere cheese producers of Normandy, offering help if it would open a plant in Wisconsin. Negotiations proceeded. I located an abandoned cheese factory in Belmont, Wisconsin, and a number of hog farms willing to use the plant's whey, a bothersome by-product of cheese making. We sealed the deal with a glass of champagne in the Speaker's hideaway in the Capitol. Besnier et Fils has successfully produced its Brie and Camembert at Belmont ever since. The happy result: more jobs for Wisconsin dairy farmers and cheese makers, more soft cheese for the nation's yuppies, and more profits for Besnier et Fils.

A similar opportunity presented itself in soy sauce. For years Kikkoman, the great Japanese sauce maker, had been importing Wisconsin soy beans to Japan, where it transmuted them into its fabled soy sauce. Shipped back over the Pacific, the sauce lubricated many a dish of American chop suey. Thus I vigorously supported Kikkoman's bid to open a soy sauce plant in Walworth, Wisconsin, close to both its source of supply and the market for its product. When last I looked, the Kikkoman plant in Wisconsin was humming. The only Japanese apparent was the plant manager, who had become the darling of the local Rotary.

AID

Aid to developing countries has been part of U.S. foreign policy ever since World War II and President Harry Truman's 1949 inaugural address with its Point Four program. I always supported foreign aid and tried to make the case for it to my constituents.

Like the little girl in the nursery rhyme, when aid was good, it was very, very good, but when it was bad, it was horrid. In Chapter 4 I deplored aid when it was bad, like giantism—loading peasant countries with huge airports, superhighways, or steel mills—and like militarism—encouraging military dictators and substituting cold war hardware for civilian aid.

On every continent I made it my business to study our aid program on the spot. My reports always stressed programs that had an effect on people, like those in education and agriculture. A trip to Colombia in 1978 uncovered some things we were doing right. My companions were Jim Megellas, the former Fond du Lac city council chairman who had helped me with the Menominee (see Chapter 5), now head of the U.S. Agency for International Development (USAID) mission in Colombia, and Frank Aukofer, reporter for the *Milwaukee Journal* and former president of the National Press Club.

In the little village of Carmen, eight thousand feet up in the Andes near the border with Ecuador, several hundred *campesinos* were building a primitive road to connect their village with an existing road six miles away. Without the road they had to trek through jungle to bring their charcoal to market. The cost of the road was $85,000, of which the USAID program paid 40 percent. Aukofer described the building of the road:

Men hacked away at the dirt with picks. Women with babies on their backs dug with shovels. Little boys pushed wheelbarrows, and tiny tots still in diapers picked up dirt and threw it off the roadway.

Huge trees, their gnarled roots exposed, had been hacked to pieces with axes— there are no saws, much less chain saws. The logs and stumps waited to be burned to make charcoal.

Giant rocks stood in the roadway where the families had dug around them. They would be hammered into small pieces later. The pieces would become ballast to keep the road from washing away in the rainy season.[3]

The campesinos invited us to dinner in their mud-and-straw hut. The *pièce de résistance* was an expensive delicacy, guinea pig. It tasted like kerosene, but we bravely choked it down. The mayor welcomed us, saying that we were the first elected officials, Colombian or American, ever to visit their village.

The little Carmen project seemed good. It made only a small dent in Latin American poverty, but at least it gave the villagers some hope.

8

The House Banking Committee

My first two decades in Congress, and on the House Committee on Banking and Currency, gave me a worm's-eye view of the seniority system, whereby committee chairmanships went automatically to the most senior member. Until 1975, when I helped break the system, I served under two entrenched southern Democratic chairs. Both were octogenarians and signers of the 1956 prosegregation Southern Manifesto.

The first, until his retirement in 1962, was Brent Spence of Kentucky, conservative in outlook, do-nothing in habit, and a believer that junior members should be seen but not heard. The second was Wright Patman of Texas, red-hot populist, foe of the big banks and the Federal Reserve, friend of the veteran and small business. His heart was in the right place, but his arbitrary practices quickly divided the committee into warring factions; the financial lobbies with the largest purses were able to exercise decisive power.

Both crusty oldsters had a redeeming grace—a sense of the ridiculous. I remember an early occasion when the banking committee was immobilized by a lengthy filibuster conducted by Rep. Abe Multer, Democrat of New York and a longtime foe of chairman Spence's. Abe's voice rising to almost a scream, he denounced the chairman's autocratic habits until, finally exhausted, he sat down. The chairman announced, "Your apology is accepted," and adjourned the meeting.

On another occasion Patman was berating his archenemy, William McChesney Martin, chairman of the Federal Reserve Board, as a delegation of visiting Daughters of the American Revolution entered the hearing room. "You're unconstitutional," Patman was shouting, a familiar charge based on his belief that Congress, not the Fed, had the constitutional power to "coin money, regulate the value thereof." The DAR ladies, delighted to hear the Constitution so vigorously defended, thereupon invited Patman to address their next meeting at Constitution Hall. The chairman accepted, and his opening words to the DAR went something like this:

It's an honor to address you ladies, because all now realize that it takes a woman to handle the money. It was not ever thus. In prehistoric Babylon, huge stone cart-wheels were the medium of exchange; it took a man to handle the money in those days. In ancient Iceland, the unit was a mighty ox; it took a man to handle the money in those days. And in early Ireland, the medium was a beautiful young slave-girl; it took a man . . .

At which point the ladies began to raise their eyebrows.

As the nation's financial institutions began changing rapidly in the 1960s and 1970s, the banking committee became increasingly irrelevant. This irked me. I had not asked for assignment to the banking committee when I arrived in 1955. Instead, I had requested Public Works, because it had jurisdiction over the St. Lawrence Seaway and I wanted to work on this prize for Milwaukee. But the reigning regional Democrat on the all-powerful Ways and Means Committee, which then governed committee assignments, was old Tom O'Brien of Chicago. Old Tom feared that I, a Milwaukeean, would start complaining about the "Chicago Water Steal," a perennial Milwaukee gripe that Chicago was taking too much water from Lake Michigan to flush its sewage down the Chicago River. So he put me on the banking committee instead. Once on, I had plenty of time to study the nation's financial institutions. So I soon became engrossed in the work of the committee and disappointed at its fecklessness.

With time on my hands, I went in for personal growth. Seeking new varieties of religious experience, I joined the House prayer group.[1] Grasping at fitness, I worked out daily in that princely perquisite, the House gym. Wanting diversity at home and abroad, I took a concentrated German course at the Naval Intelligence School.

And, just as important, I decided that my atrocious public speaking needed attention. I had the words, but the voice and the gestures defeated me. For the voice I put myself in the hands of the famed Billy Graham (the drama coach, not the evangelist) of Catholic University. This genius of the footlights had me keep a candle guttering endlessly at twenty feet, and my tones soon became almost dulcet. For the gestures I enlisted my doughty supporter, Lorna Warfield, widow of a distinguished Milwaukee physician and an acclaimed amateur actor in her own right. Lorna immediately diag-nosed my arm motions as too crabbed and confined; when I wished to embrace the crowed, she said, I should let my arms spread to their widest, not cabin them meanly. With the help of Billy and Lorna, my speaking be-came less atrocious.

TOPPLING THE SENIORITY SYSTEM

As the 1960s grew into the 1970s, I was now fourth in seniority on the banking committee, behind Chairman Patman, Bill Barrett of Pennsylvania, and Leonor Sullivan of Missouri. With the seniority system in full flower, I could see what the future held for me: by the time those who ranked me had all been called to Abraham's bosom, I might aspire to the chairmanship but with a mind now turned to watermelon seeds.

Meanwhile, an interesting new organization had been formed in the House, the Democratic Study Group (DSG). This innocuous-sounding outfit had been put together in 1957 by a number of junior Democratic members, including Stewart Udall of Arizona, John Blatnik and Eugene McCarthy of Minnesota, Frank Thompson of New Jersey, Richard Bolling of Missouri, Lee Metcalf of Montana, and me, to combat the prosegregation Southern Manifesto promulgated in March 1956 by almost every southern Democrat. (Chapter 10 describes the DSG's work for the civil rights legislation of the 1960s.)

The DSG was confronted by a southern minority that had been running things for years. Although it existed on paper, the Democratic Caucus did not dare to exercise any influence over what the party did. The Democratic Steering Committee, adopted a generation earlier, was moribund. The Rules Committee, under the tyrannical Judge Howard Smith of Virginia, bottled up whatever legislation he disliked. The seniority rule for committee chairmanships went unchallenged.

One by one, the DSG changed things. The caucus was made a place where party issues could be discussed. By 1965 it was able to eject from the party nominal Democrats like John Bell Williams of Mississippi for supporting Barry Goldwater for president. The Steering Committee was revived as the Steering and Policy Committee and became a real arm of the leadership. It was soon given the power to appoint committee members, a monopoly previously held by the Ways and Means Committee. The Rules Committee was made responsible to the Speaker in 1961, thus permitting the social and civil rights legislation of the 1960s to reach the floor.

Seniority was the last to fall. On June 29, 1970, Rep. Charles Vanik of Ohio and I introduced an amendment to the House rules to provide explicitly that the committee chair "need not be the member with the longest consecutive service on the committee." It got nowhere but at least was a line in the sand.

Toppling seniority would take a majority of determined Democrats. The near-landslide Democratic victory in November 1974, riding a tide of public disgust with Watergate, finally produced such a majority. A crowd of energetic new Democratic House members, largely replacing conservative Republicans or conservative Democrats, arrived in Washington ready for reform.

Interestingly, the banking committee had just had a role in the Watergate affair. When the Watergate burglars were apprehended on June 17, 1972, they were carrying checks from a Minnesota donor to the Republican campaign committee. The checks had found their way to Mexico and had then been cleared through a Miami bank. Ah-ha! I thought, here is just the jurisdictional connection the banking committee needs in order to get involved, because tracing the checks is clearly banking business. So I wrote Chairman Patman asking him to put his staff to work tracing the checks.

The staff did all it could. But by early August it was clear that the committee would have to subpoena Nixon administration figures to explain how the Republican Party's checks had gotten into the hands of the Watergate burglars. The administration resolved at all costs to block the Democratic majority on the committee from issuing the subpoenas. First, the administration called in its chits from several southern Democrats on whom it could always count. Then, to ensure that every Republican vote would be in the administration's favor, the administration replaced upright Bill Widnall of New Jersey—the ranking Republican and coordinator of the operation—with a younger and tougher type, Garry Brown of Michigan. Garry soon reported that the Republicans were united against the subpoenas.

But that still left the White House a couple of votes shy of being able to block the subpoenas. These were found in the persons of two wayward Democrats, one from each coast, each under investigation for white-collar crime by the Department of Justice. When the subpoenas came up for a vote in September 1972, the Republicans narrowly defeated Patman and his loyalists. Incidentally, the two Democrats remained unindicted throughout the subpoena proceedings; later the Department of Justice, full of rectitude and ingratitude, saw to it that they served time.

Had the subpoenas been issued in September 1972, the Watergate hearings and impeachment proceedings might well have been unnecessary. Nixon might have resigned months earlier than August 8, 1974. The nation would have been spared much agony.

The influx of new, post-Watergate Democrats in November 1974 gave me an opportunity to reform the seniority system when the new Congress convened in January 1975. At the Democratic off-year convention in Kansas City in December, I tested the waters with a speech suggesting that reform was afoot and received an encouraging response.

In January the Democratic Caucus was off to a good start, adopting rules that permitted a chairmanship to be voted on. I assumed that when the Steering and Policy Committee met to make its nominations, it would automatically nominate Patman for chairman of the banking committee; Patman would then run on his record. If he failed to receive a majority, I could then take my chances and run. To my surprise, the Steering and Policy Committee bypassed Patman and nominated me as the presumptive chairman.

Now the nomination went to the full caucus, and the Patmanites argued that their candidate was being ousted without his day in court. There was something to this argument, made persuasively by Patman's fellow

Texans, Jim Wright and Barbara Jordan; I went down to defeat on the first ballot. A few days later the caucus, now instructed to ask members to pick between Patman and me, favored me by a vote of 147–117. Almost all the recently elected Young Turks supported me. I thanked them for their help, declaring "I am a Young Turk sixty-two years of age!"

During subsequent biennial elections for committee chairman, I never had more than a handful of votes cast against me.

Two other entrenched committee chairmen were defeated in that 1975 caucus—Eddie Hebert of Louisiana at Armed Services and Bob Poage of Texas at Agriculture. From then on, automatic seniority was no more. In the years ahead two energetic House members from Wisconsin did some toppling of their own—Les Aspin at Armed Services in 1985 and David Obey at Appropriations in 1993.

THE BANKING COMMITTEE REBORN

Now, after twenty years, I was chairman. Churchill's motto—"In victory, magnanimity"—appealed to me. I saw to it that Wright Patman had his subcommittee, that our hearing room was named the Wright Patman Room, and that he retained as much of his old staff as he needed. Age soon took its toll, and within months we were flying down to Texarkana for the old chairman's funeral, landing at Wright Patman Airport and passing a dozen Patman landmarks on the way to the church. His son Wright Patman, Jr., succeeded him and served honorably on the committee for some years.

Energized by several new members, the House banking committee began to function. For the six years of my chairmanship I was fortunate to have as my Senate banking committee counterpart Wisconsin's Bill Proxmire. For the first time in history Wisconsin held the leadership of a major committee in both bodies. While Prox's reputation was based mainly on his watchdog surveillance over spending, and his Golden Fleece awards for dubious federal grants, he was unfailingly friendly and cooperative in our committee work. Tensions between Senate and House leaders are common, and we were lucky to avoid them. Vice President Nelson Rockefeller, a witness before us, once attempted to compliment us by saying we were very sophisticated. Prox quickly interrupted Rockefeller: "Thanks, but never call us 'sophisticated' in Wisconsin; 'smart,' sure, but never 'sophisticated.'"

In 1975 my first goal as chairman was to help Congress carry out its constitutional responsibility over money by becoming informed on Federal Reserve monetary policy. The Federal Reserve not only operated in secret but refused to inform Congress of the reason for its actions. We succeeded in passing a concurrent resolution—one not needing the president's signature but nonetheless binding on the Fed—directing the Fed chairman to appear twice yearly before the banking committee to report on financial conditions and the Fed's monetary policies.

These January and July appearances have greatly aided Congress in advising the Fed where it believes advice is needed. Thus the 1975 concurrent resolution also directed the Fed to encourage "expansion in the monetary and credit aggregates appropriate to facilitating prompt economic recovery," a directive the Fed promptly followed. Again, in June 1982 Congress in its budget resolution directed the Fed to ease money, which the Fed did, starting in August.

When I sought the committee's chairmanship, I had called for an across-the-board study of our financial system and finally got it in 1976. The FINE study ("Financial Institutions in the Nation's Economy") was headed up by two expert Californians, James Pierce of the University of California, Berkeley, and his wife, Mary Ann, who had been assistant to Federal Reserve governor Andrew Brimmer and later became California banking commissioner. Because I knew that my huge and fractious committee would be unable to agree on any meaningful statement, I called not for a committee report but a staff study, published by the committee but with the chair solely responsible for it. The FINE study made many trail-blazing recommendations, not yet enacted but in my judgment still valid. Among them: instead of banks and savings and loans, have one generalized institution; instead of spreading regulation of financial institutions over a multiplicity of agencies, set up a single agency; and instead of restricting banking activities, allow banks a wider range of services.

Three significant laws were enacted in 1977. The Community Reinvestment Act made illegal the practice of banks' redlining low-income neighborhoods and required them to consider the credit needs of the entire community if they wished regulators to let them merge, branch, or engage in interstate banking.

The Federal Reserve Reform Act applied conflict-of-interest laws to the Federal Reserve and required the twelve regional Fed banks to expand their openings for women and blacks on their boards of directors.

The International Banking Act required the numerous foreign banks operating in the United States, hitherto unregulated, to meet the same standards as domestic banks. The act also guaranteed reciprocal fair treatment by foreign governments for U.S. banks doing business abroad.

In 1978 Congress enacted the Consumer Cooperative Bank Act, designed to furnish consumers with a source of credit for food, housing, health care, and other necessities.

The 1970s had seen the erosion of New York City's financial viability. Wall Street was in the doldrums. The needle trades were fleeing the Big

Apple for the nonunion South. One after another, city administrations had simply been postponing the day of municipal bankruptcy.

New York's mayor and its financial and civic leaders appealed to Washington for a loan guarantee to tide it over while it enacted reforms. President Ford's answer to the plea was encapsulated by the *New York Daily News's* memorable headline: "Ford to NY: Drop Dead." I started an intensive study of what might be done and concluded that if state and city officials could come up with a comprehensive plan for restoring solvency to the nation's leading city, the gamble of a federal guarantee would be worthwhile. Over the months a plan emerged. The New York congressional delegation, Democrats and Republicans, took to the road to generate national support. The Carter administration was helpful. The bailout legislation passed, the city was saved, and the guarantee was never called upon.

In 1979, with the success of the New York City rescue mission, other applicants for federal aid for failing enterprises began to present themselves. Foremost among them was the ebullient Lee Iacocca, a wonderchild of the automobile industry who became Chrysler's CEO as the smallest of the Big Three started losing market share. In close harmony with the United Auto Workers, Iacocca roamed the House corridors seeking support for the government bailout.

I had doubts about the Chrysler bailout from the beginning. If Chrysler wasn't making a product people wanted to buy, why should the government step in and perhaps send good money after bad? But had the auto maker been allowed to go under, the country would have lost many thousands of jobs at Chrysler and its suppliers. Reluctantly, I supported the bill and saw it through the House floor and through the Senate-House conference. Chrysler was saved, and it did repay its loan. But the experience left me leery of an "industrial policy" in which Uncle Sam would try to pick winners among specific industrial firms.

My last major banking committee legislation came in 1980. The Federal Reserve System had always required that banks put up reserves, based on a percentage of their deposits, in order to give the Fed a base for controlling the total lending power of the banks. But the law had a big loophole: reserve requirements could be imposed only on nationally chartered banks or on such state-chartered banks as chose to be "members" of the Fed. Posting reserves was costly to the banks, because they thereby gave up their interest earnings. This bankers' contribution to the treasury, worth billions annually, was known as *seigniorage,* an ancient practice whereby kings obtained for themselves a bit of the value of the coins they minted. Now banks were leaving the Federal Reserve System in droves, 550 of them in 1978 alone, to avoid these payments to the treasury. The Fed stood in danger of losing control over monetary policy.

The Fed staff concocted a remedy: bribe the banks to stay in the Fed system by paying them interest on their reserves, a loss of several billion a year to the treasury. I objected strenuously, pointing out that this would simply increase the deficit. Instead, I proposed that all banks, whether members of the Fed or not, be subject to reserve requirements. We worked out details that were fair to both the banks and the treasury, and the Depository Institutions Deregulation and Monetary Control Act of 1980 passed and was signed into law.

What was the verdict of the banking industry on my years as chair of the banking committee? Mixed, I would have to say. An "exit interview" appeared in the *American Banker* for January 6, 1983, the day of my retirement.

Washington. Rep. Henry S. Reuss insists his lawmaking has caused "apoplexy" among the nation's bankers.

Bankers generally agree.

But in retrospect, the retired Wisconsin Democrat believes the financial community fared pretty well while he was chairman of the House Committee on Banking, Finance, and Urban Affairs.

And again bankers agree with Mr. Reuss.

But the financial world and the congressman have not always shown such harmony. Conservative bankers and the liberal Mr. Reuss often found themselves at odds over the government's role in business. . . .

Bankers perceived Mr. Reuss as an antibanking lawmaker. . . .

However, those who worked closely with Mr. Reuss insist that in practice he was not out to burden the financial institutions with strict regulations and red tape. He was merely perceived that way by lobbyists, they say. . . .

Despite past conflicts, veteran banking lobbyists agreed that few lawmakers were as sincere and knowledgeable as Mr. Reuss. The congressman himself said his decision to leave Capitol Hill was based solely on his own need for a change.

"I've loved the Congress," Mr. Reuss says. "And I am in no way disillusioned, frustrated, or burned out. But I do feel that after 28 years everybody—banker, legislator, or whatever—ought to do something new." . . .

On banking and finance matters, Mr. Reuss' proposals became crusades. "He had no interest in compromise," a bank lobbyist said of Mr. Reuss' disregard for the political aspects of lawmaking.

Tighter credit controls, greater accountability for the Federal Reserve Board, and more information disclosure by banks to their depositors were among the causes Mr. Reuss supported in the face of opposition by either bankers or regulators. . . .

Mr. Reuss saw the major bank lobbies as highly effective, except that "they tend to cancel each other out. So if you want to get something done, you just have to go ahead and do it."

And that is precisely how he conducted himself, regardless of political considerations.[2]

THE FEDERAL RESERVE SYSTEM

Established in 1913, the Federal Reserve was just coming of age when I came to the banking committee forty years later. Its record was undistinguished, to say the least. It had sat by helplessly during the great boom of the 1920s and the bust of the 1930s. During World War II it made its goal a 2 percent interest rate for the treasury's long-term bond; by 1951 continuing this target would have risked creating inflationary clouds of new money. Sen. Paul Douglas used his Joint Economic Committee position to hammer out the Fed-Treasury Accord, in which the Fed wisely gave up its wartime 2 percent mission.

Chairmanship of the Fed now passed to the brilliant young St. Louis investment banker William McChesney Martin. His guideline for Fed monetary policy—"Take away the punch bowl when the party gets rough" —worked to create a policy that was a shade on the tight side under Eisenhower and one a little looser and just about right under Kennedy and Johnson.

Under Nixon and Ford the Fed's chairman was Arthur Burns. A stellar witness before the committee, Arthur would fill the hearing room with fragrant smoke from his pipe and pacify a member who had just asked a dumb question: "Congressman, you may well be right!" I respected him very much for his willingness to look at the economy as a whole rather than cling to a narrowly conceived monetary policy.

President Carter had a chance to appoint a Fed chairman, and he named William Miller, a successful industrialist from Tenneco. We worked together constructively on the Monetary Control Act both before and after he went over to the treasury as secretary.

Paul Volcker succeeded to the Fed chairmanship in early 1979, when inflation caused mainly by OPEC's two massive oil price increases was ravaging the economy. In October 1979 he sharply tightened money and accompanied this by restricting consumer credit. This had a devastating effect. A severe recession ensued, enough to ensure that Jimmy Carter would be held to one term.

With inflation continuing, the Fed tightened money again in March 1981, raising interest rates to 20 percent as its part of Reagan's economic program. This set off a crippling recession that lasted until money was loosened in August 1982. I believe that Volcker overdid the money tightening, but his monetary sins pale against the fiscal and regulatory sins of both the Carter and Reagan administrations.

Although the Fed has a statutory duty to follow both the goal of maximum employment and that of minimum inflation, since the 1980s it has tended to overlook the former and concentrate on the latter. My sparkling friend and former staff director, James Galbraith of the University of

Texas, and I expressed our disagreement with this fixation in a piece for the *New York Times* in 1996:

For 50 years, the Federal Reserve's statutory goals have been maximum employment with minimum inflation.

The Employment Act of 1946 mandated the Fed to work toward "maximum employment, production and purchasing power. . . ." Since the 1950s, all of the Fed chairmen . . . [except] Alan Greenspan have explicitly accepted that these should be the goals of monetary policy, as they are the goals of the President and Congress.

But now Mr. Greenspan and Congressional Republicans are making it clear that they would junk this bipartisan bedrock of maximum employment and minimum inflation. The approach is embodied in legislation sponsored by Senator Connie Mack, Republican of Florida, and Representative H. James Saxton, Republican of New Jersey, leaders of the Joint Economic Committee. . . .

In practice, the Mack-Saxton bill would legitimize the Federal Reserve's actual policies in recent years. Forgetting about jobs and growth, Mr. Greenspan has made his reputation by battling at Armageddon against an increasingly invisible inflation. . . .

A result has been to anesthetize the economy at perhaps several million jobs below the attainable noninflationary level. Those extra jobs could go a long way toward combating poverty, ending the downsizing of the middle class and reducing the budget deficit.

Moreover, the stock and bond markets get jittery at the release of any new economic data because they perceive that Mr. Greenspan's Federal Reserve subscribes to the quaint idea that more jobs and stronger economic growth lead inevitably to runaway inflation. This has never been true, but it is a dangerous idea as long as the Fed believes it. . . .

It is no wonder that the Fed, having ignored its legal obligation to pursue maximum employment, now supports having that obligation abolished.

But picture this scene under the Mack-Saxton legislation: A recession has hit, millions are jobless, thousands of businesses go bankrupt, the banking system is in crisis. The Fed chairman, serene and confident, comes before Congress to announce that, with inflation at zero, the goal of the Mack-Saxton legislation has been achieved. Members of Congress, present en masse for the occasion, rise to their feet, cheering.

If you can't imagine this scene, then you understand why this legislation is a bad idea.[3]

This inflation-*über-alles* bias of the Fed is in large part the result of the bizarre structure of the twelve-member Federal Open Market Committee (FOMC), the agency that sets short-term interest rates. The 1935 law that set up the FOMC ordained that seven of its twelve members should be public officials—governors of the Federal Reserve appointed by the president and confirmed by the Senate—and five should be the presidents of five of the twelve regional Federal Reserve district banks, selected on a rotating basis. The presidents of the Federal Reserve district banks are not public officials but private citizens picked by the commercial bankers of the district. To make matters worse, the 1935 law gave the president of the New York Federal Reserve District Bank permanent membership on the FOMC, and the Chicago and Cleveland Bank presidents preferential status, thereby consigning the other nine district reserve bank presidents to second-class membership.

Obviously, the vital governmental task of monetary policy ought to be in the exclusive hands of public officials—the Fed's Board of Governors. Dispensing with the five private citizens would do more than just remove the banker bias of the FOMC. It would, for a change, comply with the Constitution, which provides (art. 1, sec. 2, clause 2) that "Officers of the United States" must be appointed by the president, by and with the advice and consent of the Senate.

One of my favorite sayings is that of Lincoln's friend Carl Schurz, later senator and interior secretary: "My country, right or wrong. If right, to be kept right. If wrong, to be set right." The FOMC is something that should be set right.

9

The City

Cities have always fascinated me. I have spent some of my happiest hours walking around London, Paris, Copenhagen, Vienna, Prague, Florence, Venice, Turin, Rio, Cartagena, Barcelona, Cuzco, Kyōto, Hong Kong, Singapore, Boston, Baltimore, New Orleans, San Francisco, Seattle. Great cities breathe excitement, cultural lightning, economic swirl.

Perhaps part of this fascination stems from frustration. After all, I tried twice to become mayor of Milwaukee, and twice came in second, to Frank Zeidler in 1948 and to Henry Maier in 1960. Thus rejected, I focused on urban issues as best I could from my vantage point in Congress.

My chairmanship of the House banking committee, which I assumed in 1977, gave me a chance. I changed the name of the committee from Banking and Currency to Banking, Finance, and Urban Affairs, and I established a new subcommittee, the Subcommittee on the City, of which I became the chair.

SUBCOMMITTEE ON THE CITY

The Subcommittee on the City had no power to create legislation. This was no great handicap, however, because what cities needed was not more laws but a broad new approach to their problems. Under our able staff director, Holly Staebler, hearings and reports flowed from the subcommittee in profusion. We heard Toronto officials tell how they had linked their new transport system with city development. Stuttgart explained how it preserved its historic center. We took a look at the British experiment with new towns such as Milton Keynes and concluded that new-towns-in-town made more sense than building distant new communities that tended to sap the strength of the beleaguered older cities.

In 1978 I sponsored an amendment enacted into law requiring the Department of Housing and Urban Development (HUD) to issue an urban policy statement every two years. The statement was to do for cities what the president's annual economic report and environmental report do for those fields. The first urban statement, in 1979, was a first-rate document. HUD was then headed by its finest leader, Patricia Harris. We had become close friends through a dear mutual friend, Jane Dahlman Ickes, a pal from my youth in Milwaukee and widow of FDR's pugnacious secretary of the interior, Harold Ickes.

The years have not dealt kindly with the urban policy statement, long forgotten until HUD secretary Andrew Cuomo vigorously revived it in 1997. Nor with the Subcommittee on the City, unceremoniously abandoned in the 1980s. Nor with the Committee on Banking, Finance, and Urban Affairs, which under the Gingrich revolution of 1995 became the Committee on Banking and Financial Services—no more urban affairs, evidently.

In my 1977 book, *To Save a City,* I set forth my idea of a model urban policy. Twenty years later its recommendations are still relevant:

- The city's clustering still offers advantages in transportation and communication. And the great institutions of the spirit still need the critical mass the city provides. In a time of scarcity, the city is the Great Conservator of land, energy and resources.
- Sprawl development is wasteful of energy in transportation, in heat loss, in the energy-intensive activity of building new facilities, and in the energy loss represented by abandoning or demolishing structures in the central city.
- We must evolve, for the first time in this country, a national urban policy. The European experience demonstrates that cities can be more livable and more likely to survive with a national urban policy than without one, and that an urban policy can and should be both multifaceted and flexible.
- The most direct and effective way to help cities is to provide jobs. Ultimately that task must be heavily assisted by the federal government. Part of our central city unemployed must be helped to go where the jobs are. Good transportation and an end to exclusionary suburban housing practices can bring the urban unemployed to jobs in the suburbs and beyond. National service jobs must be part of the process.
- The humanscale neighborhood should become the basic building block in the revival of cities. Here the impetus must come from the neighbors themselves, though they can be critically assisted by government action. Newly self-conscious neighborhoods can lobby city hall into rendering better municipal services. Rehabilitation of older homes can be accomplished for a fraction of the cost of old-style massive bulldozing and new building. Essential to the rehabilitation of neighborhoods is multiuse zoning.
- The role of the city as the Great Conservator of land, energy and re-

sources can be enhanced by city planning to encourage homes within walking, bicycling or short commuting distance of workplaces, shopping and recreation; by mass transit, including light rail, improved bus service, and restrictions on automobile use in central districts; by population shifts to bring the urban unemployed nearer jobs in suburbs and exurbs, and middle-class people back to the city in which they work; by zoning reform making for a mix of homes, jobs and shops.

- City government, hemmed in by state-imposed restrictions, has proved largely incapable of modernizing itself. Somehow, the states must be motivated to take the lead in such modernization. An obvious motivation can be provided by making federal revenue sharing with the states dependent upon the states' at least filing plans for such modernization. Here as elsewhere presidential leadership is essential.[1]

If I were asked to name one issue for the fifty states to concentrate on for the start of the twenty-first century, I would suggest *the city*. Things go in cycles. The early years of the twentieth century saw the states enact great political reforms—direct election of senators, regulation of monopolies, the initiative and referendum, workers' compensation. In Wisconsin this was the era of progressive Republican Bob La Follette. The middle years of the century saw the states battle to protect their natural resources. In Wisconsin this was the era of conservation-minded governors like Democrat Gaylord Nelson and Republican Warren Knowles.

With the twenty-first century looming, the states could well turn their energies to the plight of their local communities, with special attention to problems like these:

1. *Government in metropolitan areas.* States now need to follow the lead of New York and California a century ago in encouraging city-county mergers in New York City and San Francisco. More recently, Minnesota promoted metropolitan revenue sharing in the Twin Cities. My own city and county of Milwaukee, by the way, could save money by merging their duplicating governments.

2. *Land use.* The country cannot afford more urban sprawl. States could follow Oregon by encouraging localities to set up urban growth limits, thus concentrating development for the sake of economy and preserving open space for the sake of ecology. Or they could transfer zoning and planning functions from archaic local governments, often vulnerable to special interests, to regional planning commissions capable of a broader view. Again, Wisconsin has an instrument ready at hand in the regional planning commissions. Set up in the 1960s, they have been producing sensible plans that the local town boards frequently disregard. Chapter 13 describes my efforts in 1998 to limit sprawl in Wisconsin.

3. *School financing.* A good primary and secondary education is essential

to American democracy. Yet our system of paying for the public schools through local real estate taxes results in bizarre inequalities between schools in suburbs and in slums. The states should eliminate these inequalities. Hawaii does it by paying the full cost of local schools out of state revenues. Short of that, states ought to ensure that spending on schools in poor and wealthy districts is at least equalized.

President Jimmy Carter invited me to the White House to discuss urban policy early in his administration, in October 1977, and I jumped at the chance. I found him extremely sympathetic. In fact, his administration did more for the American city than any, before or since. Sadly, the oil price crisis and the Iranian hostage taking preoccupied the latter days of his presidency and prevented his following through on several contemplated city initiatives.

IMPROVING FEDERALISM

Cities are orphans in our federal system. Nowhere in the Constitution is *city* mentioned, nor *federalism* nor *local government* nor the word *urban*. Federalism is very much a principle that still requires some fleshing out. The division of powers between national, state, and local governments remains blurred. Local governments are the creatures of states, but states frequently fail to provide localities with government structures that are equitable, efficient, and accountable.

I wrestled with the problem of federalism several times. I started in the late 1960s when the concept of Washington's sharing its revenues with state and local government first began receiving attention. If such unrestricted aid was to be given, why not at least require state and local governments to develop plans for modernizing themselves, with particular attention to government in metropolitan areas and to the problem of poverty in our central cities? After much study I drew up an amendment to the revenue-sharing legislation of 1970, conditioning it on a good-faith state effort to draw up a long-term modern governments plan. I set this forth at length in my 1970 book, *Revenue-Sharing: Crutch or Catalyst for State-Local Government?*

My proposed Modern Governments Act (MGA) drew heavily on what I had learned from the Marshall Plan — that the cash grants were much less important than the structure of cooperation they inspired. The Marshall Plan required the beneficiary government to draw up a plan for its modernization; the MGA required each state to do so, for itself and its localities. The Marshall Plan provided for peer review of each plan, by each of the devastated countries; the MGA would have established peer review by the other state governments of each of four geographical regions, north, south, east, and west. In the Marshall Plan the donor's approval of each country's plan was conditioned on a good-faith effort overall, not on details; in the

MGA, likewise. Finally, U.S. missions supervised implementation of the Marshall Plan on a friendly basis; the MGA also provided plenty of wiggle room so long as the state was proceeding in good faith.

When revenue sharing came up for renewal in Congress in 1973, the League of Women Voters presented my modern governments plan as an amendment to revenue sharing. It met with a favorable reception from Rep. Ben Rosenthal, the New York Democrat who sponsored the bill, and was reported out by the full Government Operations Committee. But the Nixon administration, aided by alarmist state and local officials, contrived to kill the bill on the House floor.

Although revenue sharing is no more, the idea behind MGA still could be used today if Congress ever gets around to improving the federal system. Any reincarnations of the MGA should take advantage of the great forward strides made by nongovernmental organizations in the last decade (see Chapter 13). They deserve a place in any new federal structure.

A second proposal to improve the federal system came from my work on the Committee on the Constitutional System, after my retirement from Congress. Benjamin Read, former undersecretary of state, and I proposed that a national convocation be held every ten years,

with delegates to be selected in equal numbers by federal, state and local governments in a manner to be determined by Congress, to make recommendations to achieve a more cooperative, equitable, efficient, accountable and responsive federal system, under procedures requiring Congress and the state legislatures promptly to vote on each recommendation.[2]

The convocation would give local governments constitutional recognition for the first time.

MODERN TRANSPORT

My attempts to elevate the city to the status of a national problem had their spin-offs for Milwaukee. For example, I authored the Mass Transit Research Act of 1968, directing a study and report on new systems of transportation. The resulting 1969 report, *New Transport Systems,* contained a number of Jules Verne–like ideas. One of them was dual mode: a little electrically propelled cockleshell you could drive from your garage to a rail system, which would hook you on and then whisk you to within another short self-propelled ride to your office, shop, or factory. I put together a coalition of Allis-Chalmers for the propulsion, American Motors for the vehicle, and Milwaukee County for the right-of-way and got a grant for a feasibility study. But the Nixon administration ended the New Transport Systems program in 1973. So we still do not know whether dual mode would have worked.

I kept close watch on foreign technology for rapid transit and high-speed rail. With my help Congress and the Japanese Diet formed a committee to try to adapt the Japanese bullet train for U.S. needs, and another coalition of Congress and the French National Assembly tried to do the same for the French high-speed train grand vitesse (TGV).

But it was from the Germans that I learned about magnetic levitation (maglev), by which a train is lifted by magnets a fraction of an inch above a single rail and is then magnetically propelled forward on a high-speed frictionless trip. In Kassel, Germany, where the German experiment was being conducted in the 1970s, I actually piloted this wonder for a few yards. I put together another coalition, including Milwaukee County executive Bill O'Donnell, Wisconsin governor Lee Dreyfus, the Wisconsin Electric Power Company, and the Budd Company, which was affiliated with the German experimenters. Their study of a maglev between downtown Milwaukee and Chicago, with stops at the airports, was completed in 1982. It showed that if the maglev worked, the project was economically feasible and would not require the destruction of a single structure because it would use abandoned rail lines for its monorail.

Today, sixteen years later, the maglev is still just a dream. American engineers first advanced the maglev concept in the 1960s, but the United States has concentrated on new transport to outer space, leaving to others new transport on Earth. The Germans are still at it and hope to have a prototype maglev running the 180 miles from Hamburg to Berlin by 2005. I join maglev's chief U.S. supporter, the indefatigable senator Daniel Patrick Moynihan, in the hope that the United States, present at the conception of maglev, can participate in its fruition.

HOUSING AND PUBLIC WORKS

Low-income housing was another area where programs out of Washington could help Milwaukee. One such was Section 221(h), which in the late 1960s provided mortgages at 1 percent interest for low-income working families. George Pazik, a former Schusters' department store official with an oversize social conscience, had set up Northside Citizens Neighborhood Conservation Corporation (NCNCC), a nonprofit with an office in Milwaukee's largely black central city. NCNCC was into all manner of good works but lacked a housing component. George and I formed a partnership to rehabilitate rundown but sturdy neighborhood homes for sale on those splendid 1 percent mortgage terms to qualified working families. We engaged two young eager beavers, Dennis Conta and Richard Weening, to run the operation. We bought up several hundred homes, fixed them up, and sold them to proud new home owners.

Large-scale projects were another congressional specialty. I am aware of the criticism of pork-barrel construction but of course insist that all of mine were useful and economical. The first was a twofer in 1962, involving the new central post office and the neighboring new Amtrak station in downtown Milwaukee. The project needed approval from the Post Office. Postmaster General Edward Day signed off on the project from a railroad coach parked at the old Milwaukee Road railway station, which was slated for demolition. He later gently complained to me that he felt like the German general in World War I who was compelled to surrender in the railway car at Compiègne, France.

There followed the Federal Reserve Center, on Broadway; the Harbor Bridge, joining my district with that of Representative Zablocki; the Veterans' Domiciliary at Wood, Wisconsin; and finally the Federal Office Plaza, part of the Grand Avenue downtown redevelopment.

DOWNTOWN AND NEIGHBORHOODS

By the mid-1970s the city of Milwaukee, with broad business support, had on the drawing boards a tax incremental district plan for its west-of-the-river downtown. The once-proud downtown had become a desert of shuttered shop windows, graffiti-scarred buildings, and adult bookstores. The tax incremental plan included a festival marketplace, with adequate parking, to revivify the area. The public costs of this giant project were to be paid for by the incremental taxes that would accrue to the city from the new construction. But there was a difficulty: the added tax values created by the project were not quite enough to finance it. I had already floated the idea of a new federal building to house the various federal offices then scattered over about thirty downtown locations, many of them inadequate. Suddenly, the proposed new federal office building and its tax base (it was built by private developers and leased to the federal government for thirty years) became the key that could unlock the downtown project.

I issued a white paper in early 1975 that backed both the downtown renewal and the renewal of a large neighborhood, which had come to be known as Park Freeway West. The land for the proposed Park Freeway West had been cleared some years before, demolishing hundreds of homes and destroying the area, but the freeway idea had been abandoned. Now I urged that the area be designated for decent housing, job-creating industry, garden plots, playing fields, and a farmers' market. The city set up a planning group composed of neighborhood people to oversee the project.

Both projects were successful. Park Freeway West has become a new town in town and is acting as a magnet for neighboring blocks. The Federal Office Plaza houses not only the federal establishment but a number of private tenants. In front of the building is a massive piece of outdoor sculpture by Helaine Blumenfeld, a gifted young historian who worked on my

Washington staff and later became one of Britain's foremost artists. Her construct of five massive blocks of Norwegian granite invites public use, particularly by sportive children.

For several years in the late 1970s, while planning for the Park Freeway West renewal was still in progress, I sponsored on a couple of empty blocks the "Small Is Beautiful" exposition. Entirely the work of neighborhood people, the exhibit featured an electricity-generating windmill, an electric automobile, photovoltaic cells in action, and some prize-winning garden plots.[3]

10

Equal Rights

The great philosophical idea that burst upon human consciousness two hundred years ago was equality. Thomas Jefferson put it into the Declaration of Independence. Abraham Lincoln embedded it in the Gettysburg Address. The idea has spread around the world. Every July 4, at twenty speeches in as many parks, I would recall our national heritage of equality.

But our Constitution reflects the reality of its time. It does not mention equality. Instead, Indians, blacks, and women were nonpersons in our basic document.

Succeeding generations made some tries at redressing this original sin. Indian rights became the subject of scores of halfhearted Indian treaties. The Thirteenth, Fourteenth, and Fifteenth Amendments outlawed slavery and expanded civil liberties. The Nineteenth Amendment gave women the vote in 1920.

DISCRIMINATION

But the stain of discrimination was not removed. Indians were robbed of their lands despite the paper treaties. (Chapter 5 describes my attempts to redress the balance for Wisconsin's Menominee.) African Americans were still subjected to endless inequities, legal and illegal. Women were still in many respects second-class citizens.

The period from 1948 to 1968 saw great advances in equality in our country, advances in which I was proud to play a small role.

The population of my Milwaukee district was at least 20 percent African American, and these constituents were always among my strongest supporters. Beyond merely responding to a "constituent interest," I felt deeply that their cause was a righteous one. Something my old friend Bill Cary of my bachelor days (see Chapter 2) had said to me years before had stuck in my mind as a good precept: "You know," he said, "the American Negro has suffered so much so stoically for so long I want in my life to see whether I can't do something to make things better."

The momentous civil rights legislation in voting, accommodations, and housing was a high point in government's golden age. It had its origins in 1948, when Harry Truman desegregated the military and then championed the successful efforts of Sen. Hubert Humphrey and Rep. Andrew Biemiller of Wisconsin to put a strong civil rights plank in the Democratic platform.

Because I was not a member of the Judiciary Committee, I could not participate directly in shaping these laws. But the Democratic Study Group played a vital role in all of them. The regular Democratic whip organization, deeply plagued with boll weevils, obviously could not be relied on to keep the troops on the House floor to ward off crippling amendments. So we self-appointed whips from the DSG kept the vigil, and the Civil Rights Act of 1964, the Voting Rights Act of 1965, and other landmarks of civil rights were all enacted.

One opportunity for more direct involvement did present itself. In the mid-1960s a case involving discrimination in housing, *Mayer v. St. Louis*, was about to be argued before the Supreme Court. A large developer was being sued for excluding African Americans from his housing development, and the government was weakly resting its case on the ground that discrimination was illegal because a large development resembled a city — a position that would have let escape the great majority of housing discrimination cases. With some superb staff help I found a forgotten but still valid 1866 law that expressly forbade any discrimination in housing. I presented this statute in my brief as a friend of the court. Justice William O. Douglas used it as the basis for his concurring opinion knocking down the discrimination.

The guiding star of the civil rights movement was the Reverend Dr. Martin Luther King, Jr. At the Lincoln Memorial on August 28, 1963, I was among the quarter million who heard his electrifying "I Have a Dream" speech. On April 4, 1968, King was murdered in Memphis. That night in Washington a riot, which soon spread to about 130 other cities, engulfed the nation's capital in flame and smoke. At home we heard the call for lawyers to represent the thousands arrested for looting and burning who were overflowing the bull pen at the central court. I was a lawyer, and I hurried to the courthouse. There I was assigned to defend a suspect who had been arrested with a bag of groceries in front of a burning food store. He had a receipt for the groceries, I pleaded him not guilty, and he was acquitted. My duties completed, I drove him home through several miles of milling mobs and burning buildings.

Back in my Milwaukee district, I made homes, jobs, and opportunity for the central city a priority. In Chapter 9 I described the effort to help low-income families acquire decent homes. My staff and I were busy organizing seminars for minority small businesses, helping a minority bank stay in business, and aiding central-city neighborhood organizations to grow.

Homelessness became endemic under the Reagan administration. The spectacle of thousands of newly homeless citizens opened America's eyes to the growing inequality. I helped out at Mitch Snyder's homeless shelter near the Capitol and in 1985 appeared before the House Public Works Committee to protest the Reagan administration's broken promise to make it a model shelter. This was my testimony:

I appear here to urge the Administration to keep its promise, made last November 4, to renovate the crummy, run-down, rat-infested shelter at Second and D Streets, N.W., "into a model physical shelter to house the homeless in the District of Columbia to be used as long as a critical need exists, with special attention to preserving the dignity of the homeless."

I know something about the shelter because my wife and I—mostly my wife—have been helping out in the clothing, laundry, counseling, and other departments of the shelter. As a result, we have come to admire the volunteers who have kept the shelter going since January 1984. We have seen them overcome difficulties beyond imagining in providing shelter for some eight hundred men and women who have lost their jobs, or never had a job, or were turned out by Saint Elizabeth's or some other mental institution, or have been dispossessed of their homes by the marshal—some saints, some sinners, but all fellow-Americans down on their luck.

Having made its promise on November 4, 1984, the Administration for many months has been sitting on a dime, doing nothing. Last May the Administration revealed its "plans." Its "shelter"—four barn-like rooms each to house two hundred people—would have been rejected for a 16th century almshouse. . . .

And there the matter rests, with the GSA now threatening to tear down the building, and the U.S. District Court, in *The Shelter v. Ronald Reagan,* pondering the legalities of it all.

Legalities aside, a word needs to be said about the rights and wrongs of the matter. They're quite simple: when the government makes a solemn promise—to get rid of the rats and to provide a "model shelter"—it ought to keep its promise.

'A public promise is on a higher plane, if anything, than a private one. . . . If people today are increasingly cynical about the integrity of government, it is because they perceive government as playing fast and loose with its promises.

Happily, the Reagan administration shortly did keep its promise to repair the center, thanks largely to the vigorous internal lobbying of Sarah Baker, the wife of Chief of Staff James Baker.

Women too were victims of discrimination, more subtle than that experienced by Native Americans or African Americans but discrimination nonetheless. During the 1960s women revolted not only against war and racism but against sex discrimination.

Like most other American males, I was guilty of my share of discrimination against women. Without much thought, I assigned to Margaret most of the parenting and homemaking, retaining the responsibility of breadwinning. When I was transferred early in my army career from Camp Van Dorn in Mississippi to Washington, D.C., I automatically assumed that she would love to give up her job as an investment analyst in Chicago to make the move. Years later, when I was in Congress, I continued to see her as a homemaker-parent, as well as a gracious congressional wife. To her credit, by the early 1960s she broke out of this straitjacket—she completed her doctoral degree at George Washington University and became head of the economics department at the University of the District of Columbia. Looking back, women's rights was an issue I should have backed much earlier at home.

Home aside, my record on women's rights was reasonable enough. My most effective efforts were after I had acquired some clout as chairman of the banking committee. The Federal Reserve Reform Act of 1977 required the Federal Reserve banks to open their directorships to women and minorities. Our committee report on the bill of August 2, 1977, objected to "the virtual exclusion of women, blacks, and representatives of labor unions, consumer interest organizations, and non-managerial and non-producer groups. Currently, for example, out of 108 Reserve Bank directors only 4 are women and only 3 are minority persons." Today, twenty-one years later, representation for women and African Americans at the Fed has greatly increased. Another measure enacted in 1976 made it easier for married women to obtain credit in their own names.

ECONOMIC INEQUALITY

Sadly, as legal inequality against this or that group in our society has been lessening, inequality of income and wealth has been increasing. Today our inequality of incomes is the worst in the industrialized world. In the last twenty years the share of income held by the top 20 percent of American families has risen 13 percent, while that of the bottom 20 percent has fallen by 22 percent and that of the middle 60 percent has stagnated.

During this time the number of American households making $1 million a year has multiplied five times in stable dollars. And two-thirds of these huge incomes come from the portfolios of these households, largely stocks and bonds, rather than from employment. In 1997 a Democratic president signed a budget bill proffered by a Republican Congress that lowered the capital gains and estate taxes on these portfolios and thus increased the inequality that is gnawing at our society.

I took every opportunity I could to document the dangers to American democracy of this growing inequality. Economically, it could lead to a shortfall in the consumer demand necessary to keep the economy growing. Recessions come when too many goods chase too few consumers. Improving the purchasing power of the lowest one-third of American households seems like a sensible approach to ensure prosperity, not only for those at the bottom but for those at the top.

Socially, as I pointed out in a 1984 speech in Philadelphia to the Henry George Association, inequality weakens the social contract that makes democracy possible:

The effects of inequality are social as well as economic. People think of equality as just some abstract idea until they see their shares of income and wealth worsen. As the gap widens between high-income investors, lawyers, accountants, executives and low-income filling station attendants, hospital orderlies, fast food operators, tension enters the garden of Eden. An American plutocracy that consumes conspicuously, monopolizes wealth and power, controls the media, and buys elections is not a pleasant prospect.

Jefferson, we are here. Equality is once more an issue for the times.

In the early Republic few were wealthy and few were poor. Wealth and income were distributed equitably. As Benjamin Franklin observed:

There are few great proprietors of the soil and few tenants; most people cultivate their own lands, or follow some handicraft or merchandise; very few are rich enough to live idly on their rents or incomes or to pay the high prices given in Europe [for works of art].

In 1839 Emerson submitted that the just person would favor "facilitating in every manner the access of the young and poor to the sources of wealth and power."

But after the Civil War, the industrial revolution and the opening of the West soon brought about great economic disparity. Industry, mining, lumber, railroads, and finance made both multimillionaires and the masses of workers who lagged behind. Chief Justice Edward G. Ryan of the Wisconsin Supreme Court pointed out in 1873, "The accumulation of individual wealth seems to be greater than it ever has been since the downfall of the Roman Empire. . . . For the first time in our politics, money is taking the field as an organized power."

Progressive political leaders like William Jennings Bryan of Nebraska, Robert La Follette of Wisconsin, and Presidents Theodore Roosevelt and Woodrow Wilson undertook to arrest this worsening economic inequality in the early years of the twentieth century. As TR said at Osawatomie, Kansas, in 1910, "I mean not merely that I stand for fair play under the present rules of the game, but that I stand for having those rules changed so as to work for a more substantial equality of opportunity and of reward for equally good service."

But the modest gains in equality during the progressive era were wiped out by the boom and bust of the 1920s. It remained for the New Deal and World War II to promote improvements in the distribution of income and wealth and thus usher in the golden age of 1948–1968, when economic equality was at its fairest.

What could be done to rein in the move of the last twenty years toward greater economic inequality?

With respect to the ballooning share of income and wealth for those at the top, we can hope that the private market will eventually provide the corrective machinery. Star athletes and entertainers will continue to command the huge incomes with which consumers wish to reward them. But markets are capable of checking those corporate executives who enjoy rewards that depend not on their uniqueness but on their ability to staff their governing boards with compliant directors who vote them outsize salaries, bonuses, stock options, and golden parachutes. Already, some large pension funds are beginning to blow the whistle on runaway executive compensation. It might be useful for some of the large mutual funds to join in the policing.

Although the government probably can do little to decrease the swollen shares of income and wealth at the top, it at least should avoid measures that increase it. For example, the 1997 reduction in the capital gains tax rate from 28 percent to 20 percent benefits mainly the top one-fifth of households that most enjoyed the stock market boom of the 1980s and 1990s. And the 1997 decision to increase the estate tax exemption from $600,000 to $1 million simply gives dynastic heirs even more of a head start over the rest of the nation. Progressive income and estate taxes are the two great equalizers of our federal system. We should be simplifying them and plugging their loopholes, not systematically weakening them and thus creating greater inequality.

Ironically, it may be the monolithic devotees of free markets at all social costs who have inadvertently helped to lessen inequality. The Federal Reserve, for example, while recognizing that the stock market was " 'irrationally exuberant" in late 1996 when the Dow was at 6,000, failed to use its power to contain bank margin lending for stock speculation ("mustn't interfere with free markets"), allowing the Dow bubble to climb to 9,300 in July 1998, before it burst. This surrender to speculation may turn out to have cost the upper 20 percent of American households enough wealth and income to measurably decrease inequality. As the poet William Cowper observed, God moves in a mysterious way, His wonders to perform!

But most of the effort to arrest the move toward greater inequality must lie in improving the lot of the average household. For workers at the lower end of the income scale, expansion of the Earned Income Tax Credit; sharply reducing the present Social Security payroll tax on the working poor; working for international labor, social welfare, and environmental standards; pegging the minimum wage to increases in the cost of living; expanding health, housing, education, training, and child care programs; and a reinvigorated labor movement would all help. Above all, we should remember JFK's dictum that a rising tide lifts all ships. Stronger growth in the economy, subject to environmental limitations, helps everybody. Improving the purchasing power of the working poor can be sold politically if its appeal is couched not just in terms of compassion but as a means of maintaining overall prosperity.

MY FAMILY

In civil rights and liberties I was clearly outdone by my family, who followed their feelings about race, poverty, and peace with much greater intensity. This brought them into some modest inner conflict: they did not want to harm my political career or to estrange themselves from a kindly but shaky father figure. They walked the tightrope gracefully.

From 1968 to 1989 we lived in a 1791 house in Harbor Square, in Washington's Southwest quadrant, an area that had just been "redeveloped." This misguided early venture in urban renewal involved razing the modest two-story homes of thousands of poor blacks, Irish, and Jews and erecting on their sites high-rise public housing projects for the poor and luxury condos and apartments for the well-to-do.

In those years Margaret regarded Washington as a community in need of her full participation. She served on several municipal commissions, including the District of Columbia Tax Revision Commission and the Housing Finance Agency. She was active in the Southwest Assembly, which sought to create understanding between the white and wealthy and the black and poor of Southwest. Working with our neighbor Arvonne Fraser (wife of Minnesota representative Don Fraser), she helped start a much-needed day care center and a community arts festival.

The assembly fought hard to build moderate-income homes for the missing middle in Southwest on a large vacant lot called Parcel 76. But the real estate lobby blocked the proposal, and Parcel 76 remains a parking lot.

In 1968 thousands of poor people from around the country, mostly African Americans, marched to Washington and encamped at Resurrection City on the Mall near the Lincoln Memorial. Our home at Harbor Square nearby became the place to get a shower and do your laundry for the bedraggled Milwaukee contingent under Father James Groppi. Margie was carrying a hamper of neatly folded laundry back to Resurrection City, where she was accosted by a marcher: "Lady, how much to press my pants?" "Why, nothing at all." "Lady, how do I know I'd get them back?"

The relentless Vietnam War was another of Margaret's deep concerns. In April 1967 she went up to New York City to take part in a peace parade, accompanied by her friends Scottie Lanahan, daughter of F. Scott Fitzgerald, and Lubie Pearson, wife of columnist Drew Pearson. They marched decorously, oblivious that a mile away some other protesters were proceeding to burn the flag. A day later in Washington, Rep. Glenn Davis, Republican of Waukesha, issued a statement condemning "a congressman's wife" for burning the flag. Asked by the press who this lady might be, Davis named Margaret. For this dubious accusation Davis was splendidly chastised by Miles McMillan in the Madison, Wisconsin, *Capital Times:*

There was a time when Rep. Glenn Davis represented the second congressional district in the House of Representatives and The Capital Times had to take the responsibility of checking his reckless opportunism. Now he represents the ninth district and the Milwaukee Journal has the dreary duty of watching him. The Journal checked him the other day on his blast at the wife of Rep. Henry Reuss, Milwaukee Democrat, for her part in the recent peace demonstration in New York. Incensed at the flag and draft card burning at the affair, Davis cut loose at Mrs. Reuss' part "in such a disgraceful demonstration." The Journal noted that in the huge throng (some say a quarter of a million turned out) Mrs. Reuss didn't participate in, much less see, these idiotic acts.

She was there because she believes, with millions of patriotic Americans, that the war is a tragic mistake. . . . Mrs. Reuss is a gracious and charming lady, a splendid mother of a wonderful family, an outstanding citizen and a genuine patriot. All who know her will ask with the Journal, "Who is Davis to question her loyalty by snide implication?"

Who is Davis? Davis has always been a quick draw man on anyone who stands in his way. A couple of years ago, when he was out of office and making a living the hard way, someone got in his way and he wrote him a letter saying that the person was acting like a "Jewish bill collector." When a spokesman for a Jewish group remonstrated against the obvious anti-semitism in the remark he called the protestor a "professional Jew." But he apologized when it was all made public. In 1956, when Sen. Alexander Wiley stood in his way by running for re-election to the Senate, Davis, who opposed him in the primary, attacked him for speaking at Israel bond drives.[1]

Our son Mike, eighteen in the summer of 1965, his sophomore year at Stanford, went down to Mississippi as a freedom worker to register voters and to teach children to read and write. There, in Clay County, he was frequently jailed and, in early August, charged with manslaughter after a sheriff's deputy who was searching him died of a heart attack. The news reached me at Warwick, England, and I was on the next plane back to the States and to Mississippi.

On arriving in Clay County, I found that the manslaughter charge had been dismissed and that Mike was free. So I spent the next days surveying conditions among black schoolchildren in the county. Ten years after the Supreme Court's decision in *Brown v. Board of Education* outlawing segregation, Mississippi's schools were still not only segregated but the black schools were miserable. I attended a meeting at Mt. Zion Church to hear firsthand from the children and their parents about conditions at nearby Beasley School, a combined elementary and high school for about six hundred children. On my return to Washington, I reported to the House what I had seen:

The school on the outside does not look bad. It is what goes on inside that is appalling.

Children through grade school and high school are being taught with almost no schoolbooks. The schoolbooks they have are hand-me-downs from the white school, antiquated and with many pages missing. In the high school biology class with thirty students, a fourteen-year-old girl told me that there were only three biology books, with many missing pages.

I tried out a number of eight- and nine-year-old children on reading, and found they could read numbers but not words. There are no courses offered in the elementary skills that would occur to one as desirable in a Mississippi high school—farming or mechanics for the boys; stenography, cooking, sewing, or home economics for the girls. The science classes have practically no equipment. There is no microscope, no chemistry materials, no Bunsen burner. One twenty-three-year-old graduate of the high school reported that he was totally unprepared for his college science course.

The school lacks a full-time janitor. . . . Many of the janitorial services are performed under compulsion by the students as punishment.

The parents have attempted to form a parent-teacher association, but the school board has discouraged it and forbidden a PTA to meet at the school. . . .

There is no cafeteria, no library, and no gymnasium. The playground equipment consists of one swing. The roof leaks. There are not enough desks, and some of the children have to use folding chairs to write on. In one classroom, designated for thirty students, some fifty-nine sit. The school is inadequately heated in winter. Sessions of the school are also held in July and August, so as to "free" the students for cotton picking in the fall when the school is closed. There is no protection against the heat, which is overpowering, by fans or anything else.

Senators Proxmire and Nelson made touching speeches on the Senate floor praising Mike. And the *Washington Post* published an editorial, "By Valor and Arms":

Young Michael Reuss' adventures as a civil rights worker trying to help Negroes vote in Mississippi make the State sound like part of the Congo. He was arrested for taking part in a protest demonstration and then charged with manslaughter after a highway patrol investigator died of an apparent heart attack while searching him. He was released when his father, Congressman Henry S. Reuss, of Wisconsin, flew to his support. Then a house where his lawyer and some companion civil rights workers took shelter was made the target of a succession of shotgun blasts early Sunday morning. Respect for human life appears to be at about as low an ebb as respect for the law in Mississippi.

Representative Reuss, who flew to Mississippi from economic discussions in England as soon as he heard of his son's arrest, made it clear that his trip was not intended "to procure special treatment for him. I am sure he will want to take his chances along with other civil rights workers." The sentiment does honor alike to father and son; but one can hardly escape anxiety regarding the chances of civil rights workers in Mississippi these days.

Mississippians ought to recognize the sentiment which sent Michael Reuss to their State and which prompts him to remain there in spite of peril. It is a sentiment which has ennobled the history of the Nation of which Mississippi is a part. It has its roots in a sense of responsibility for one's fellow men—the indispensable condition of democracy—and in an unwillingness to be pushed around or to see other people pushed around. Mississippians ought to understand this. The motto of their State is: "By Valor and Arms." Michael Reuss is helping to carry that motto into effect for them.[2]

A few years after Mike had involved me in a new insight into the civil rights movement, our daughter Jackie provided me a lesson in the violation of civil liberties. In late 1970 Jackie was a senior, majoring in French at Swarthmore College outside Philadelphia, having taken her junior year at the French universities of Avignon and Nanterre.

She was set to graduate in June 1971, and I had accepted an invitation from Swarthmore president Robert Cross to give the commencement address. Jackie was not enthusiastic about my role, because she well remembered how I had bombed as a speaker at her high school graduation four years before. Addressing her graduating class at Sidwell Friends' School in Washington, I had sought to identify with my audience by referring to the then-current phenomenon of hippies. Unfortunately, the word that came out of my mouth was *hippers,* causing the graduates to dissolve in laughter.

In early November 1970 a Mr. David Bowers, who exhibited his badge as an FBI agent, appeared in my office and told me that the FBI was "investigating" Jackie; he refused to say for what. It was FBI policy, he said, to inform members of Congress of any investigations of members of their family. He told me that I shouldn't worry, because the investigation had so far turned up nothing and would shortly be completed. He assured me that he would notify me when that occurred and advised me that I was not to make public his visit to me. I received all this in silence, mystified but confident that the investigation would come to nothing. Several weeks later Bowers notified me that the FBI investigation had been completed and had revealed nothing derogatory.

There the matter rested for awhile. In Tokyo on my way to a meeting of the Asian Development Bank, I got a call on April 10, 1971, from the Associated Press in Washington, asking for my comment. It seems that the FBI office in Media, Pennsylvania (near Swarthmore), had recently been burglarized by an outfit calling itself the Citizens' Committee to Investigate the FBI, which had just released to the press FBI files relating to Jackie's "investigation." The files showed FBI inquiries of the Swarthmore registrar's office, various police departments, and credit bureaus—none of them disclosing anything derogatory. Jackie was quoted as saying she thought the investigation was probably because of her antiwar beliefs and those of her family. I told the AP, "The FBI has an important responsibility to investigate crime. Its mission is not to compile dossiers on millions of Americans, Congressman's daughters or not, who are accused of no wrongdoing. They should stick to their mission."

On returning to Washington, I asked the FBI for reports that would reveal why it had investigated Jackie in the first place. The bureau refused, saying this would be contrary to its policy.

The incident sparked a national controversy on the FBI's methods. I received hundreds of letters, about evenly divided between those praising J. Edgar Hoover and denouncing me ("I wouldn't fault J. Edgar for keeping an eye on you and your children") and the reverse ("I hope your daughter will continue to work for peace and will not be deterred by harassment").

Other congressional voices were heard. On April 14, 1971, Sen. Edmund Muskie of Maine denounced the FBI for conducting surveillance on an Earth Day rally at the Washington Monument, where he had spoken. Muskie asked:

If there was widespread surveillance of Earth Day, is there any political activity in the United States which the FBI doesn't consider a legitimate subject for watching? If anti-pollution rallies are a subject of intelligence concern, is anything immune? Is there any citizen involved in politics who is not a potential subject for an FBI dossier?

On April 22 House Majority Leader Hale Boggs of Louisiana in a floor speech accused the FBI of wholesale violations of the right to privacy, including wiretapping him, and of "surveillance on the children of Members of Congress as . . . in the case of the lovely daughter of Congressman Henry Reuss." He called for Hoover's retirement.

There was still the matter of my scheduled Swarthmore commencement address, now just a few weeks off. I was disturbed that even the liberal Quaker Swarthmore had succumbed to the cold war fever to the point that some of its employees had become FBI informers, albeit without the knowledge of college officials. So I called President Cross and tried to beg off from my commencement commitment but yielded when he told me the invitations to hear me had already gone out. But I felt I had to say *something* about the investigation. So on commencement day, to the graduating class in the college's rose garden, I started out: "Members of the Class of 1971, let me first bring you greetings from a leading figure in Washington, 'Heartiest congratulations to all. Please be assured that I shall be watching over each and every one of you all the days of your lives. J. Edgar Hoover.'"

That was my last word to Hoover. His last word to me, at about the same time, came to light ten years later when I obtained my FBI file after I requested it under the Freedom of Information Act. On my file J. Edgar had written, "Reuss is just another permissive parent trying to 'cover' for his daughter. Do not have any personal contact with Reuss." The FBI, I have to report, has faithfully obeyed the director's directive for the past quarter-century, to our mutual benefit.

Our other children also put their dad to shame in the battle for civil rights and liberties.

Our eldest son, Chris, who died in a kayaking accident in 1986, became a crusader for two groups that had been laboring under an undeserved stigma, epileptics and the mentally ill. In his early thirties Chris had been diagnosed as suffering from epilepsy. After a struggle he found a stabilizing medication. He was quite public about his handicap and as a director of the Washington Epilepsy Association fought for an end to stigmatization.

As a Washington lawyer, he welcomed appointments by the court as guardian for the mentally ill, many of them in St. Elizabeth's Hospital. For his clients he was more friend and counselor than mere legal guardian. He lobbied hard for a change in public attitude toward the mentally ill.

Our youngest daughter, Anne, not to be outdone, was also a battler for civil rights and liberties. Deciding after her freshman year that the University of Wisconsin had nothing more to teach her, she went to Chicago and got a job in a factory that made plastic cups. It was a dangerous workplace, with frequent fires from the hot wax. The workers, mostly immigrant women, were cowed and without union representation. Anne decided that the plant needed a union and determined to organize one. To obtain a National Labor Relations Board election on whether to install a union, she needed to sign up at least 30 percent of her bargaining unit. But whenever she did so, the company would bring in enough new immigrant workers to invalidate the percentages. Finally, she was fired for her activities and had to abandon the campaign. Thereafter the company summoned the Immigration and Naturalization Service inspectors, complaining, "Shocking, shocking! Some illegals seem to have sneaked into our plant. Please come and deport them at once!"

Such were some of the contributions of my family. Like so many others in those days, they had their own ways of working toward greater social and economic equality in our country.

11

Serving Constituents

"Here, sir, the people rule," said the Founders, describing the close relationship they expected members of the House of Representatives to maintain with their constituents. As a member, I tried to keep in touch with the
citizens of my district, not just on matters of substantive legislation but on
their personal problems with their government.

My files were filled with thousands and thousands of constituent cases.
Social Security, veterans' affairs, immigration, small business, and taxation
were among the principal categories. Many wrote or called our Milwaukee
or Washington offices about problems involving not the federal government but state or local government, or even private matters. Rather than
bucking them to some other official, we often took a stab at handling them
ourselves. "Never say, 'Nothing can be done'" was our motto.

How various, and how bizarre, these problems were. Let me recall
some of them.

FOUR CASES

Members of the Liedertafel, one of Milwaukee's oldest German singing
societies, called me one day in 1962, very upset. They had arranged for
a concert tour of Germany and for a charter flight to carry them there.
Suddenly, the Civil Aeronautics Board (CAB) had denied them a charter,
on the incredible ground that they had not proved themselves a legitimate
cultural organization, as the charter statute required. This was devastating
news, because the Liedertafel's modest members could never have afforded
full transatlantic fares.

What to do? I called for a full-scale hearing by the CAB. The singers,
one hundred strong, arrived in Washington the night before, and we
promptly went into rehearsal. I opened the hearing by announcing to the
CAB that the Liedertafel was as professional a group as any in the land and
offered to entrust our case to the testimony of the board's own ears. The

Liedertafel then started out with a little number we had crafted the night before, to the tune of "O! Tannenbaum":

> O Mighty Board, O Mighty Board,
> How Just are Thy Decisions!

There followed a recital of German *Lieder* of unbelievable beauty. The CAB, needless to say, approved the charter without leaving the dais.

Then there was the protracted case of the men's room at the Hilltop postal station in Milwaukee. In the late 1950s the postal workers had come to me with a problem. Postal regulations required inspectors to use a peephole to observe workers in their toilet cubicles, to apprehend those who might have rifled a letter and wanted to flush away the incriminating envelope. My constituents objected, not to the inspection but to the lack of doors on the cubicles, which exposed them to the neighboring lunchroom whenever the door opened. For two years—by personal visit, letter, and telegram—I pursued the postal authorities in Milwaukee, in the regional office in Minneapolis, and in the head office in Washington. Finally, after I had threatened to do it myself, they installed the simple plywood doors that we had for so long been requesting.

Back in 1975 a Milwaukee couple appealed to me about their son. Stationed at a U.S. radar tracking station in Ethiopia, he had been kidnaped by Eritrean rebels who were fighting the Ethiopian army. There was something to be said for the Eritrean position, because Ethiopia had grabbed Eritrea in 1962 while the rest of the world, including the United States, looked the other way. Now we were sending arms to the Ethiopian dictator, ostensibly to be used against Russia, but they actually were being employed against the Eritrean nationalists.

Invited to my office, officials from the Departments of State and Defense said they could not negotiate with the Eritrean rebels for the return of my constituent. Because I became convinced that the Eritrean cause was just, on January 27, 1976, I wrote a letter to Osman Saleh Sabbe, the leader of the Population Liberation Front, telling him of my belief in his cause:

I have examined my country's policies in Ethiopia, and I am highly critical of them. I believe that there are strong historical, legal, and moral arguments for Eritrean independence, and I am particularly outraged by the press reports I have seen about the Ethiopian government's use of American equipment for repression of the independence movements.

I have urged my views upon Secretary of State Henry Kissinger, and I have suggested that the Kagnew Communications Unit be closed and that American military assistance to Ethiopia be terminated. I have also been expressing that point of view to my colleagues in the U.S. Congress. . . . Frankly, however, I find considerable resistance among Members of Congress, and it arises from the very fact that American citizens are being held captive. The senseless punishment which has been visited on them and on their families creates resentment and a reluctance to consider any change in U.S. policies as long as these men are being held hostage. . . .

The time has come for a humanitarian and generous action on the part of Eritrean leaders to free the U.S. captives. That action would focus world attention much more favorably on your cause, and it would certainly help me and others who feel as I do in our efforts to terminate misguided policies of military aid to Ethiopia, and to make sure that a fair share of food aid reaches Eritrea.

Osman replied on February 19, 1976, that his Popular Liberation Front did not indulge in kidnapping innocent people, that he was grateful for my support of Eritrea, and that my constituent would shortly be released. The promise was kept, and within weeks my constituent was safely on his way home to Milwaukee and his parents.

Another case, in the late 1960s, required that I go into U.S. District Court in Milwaukee to represent a constituent. He was a middle-aged Italian American with a sad tale to tell. Many years before, during World War II, he had been drafted into the army from his home in Upper Michigan. One day, at camp in Alabama, the commanding officer had come through and "requisitioned" several score of GIs, including my man, who had had peacetime mining experience in Michigan's Keweenaw Peninsula, to work as copper miners at the regular GI wage of a pittance. This was supplemented at war's end with a $1,000 severance bonus. Years later, and unbeknown to my constituent, the army secured default judgments for the bonus, plus interest, claiming it was paid by mistake. Now the government was trying to collect on these judgments in federal court in Milwaukee, where my man now lived.

I appeared on his behalf and spoke my objections to the assistant U.S. attorney who was handling the case. He suggested that perhaps something could be arranged and that we go in and see his boss, the U.S. attorney. Sitting opposite, I noticed that the assistant had slipped a note to his boss. It lay on the boss's desk, facing away from me. Having a certain facility for reading upside down, I observed that the note said, "Let's steal Reuss' thunder," and recommended a quiet settlement that would not affect the numerous similar lawsuits the army was bringing against other dragooned copper miners. My client was exonerated, and I insisted that the government's position be made a matter of record and that the other lawsuits should also be dismissed.

AN OMBUDSMAN FOR AMERICA

The present system of vigorous constituent representation is less than ideal. For one thing, it means that each of the 535 members of Congress maintains a staff of caseworkers, obviously not as efficient as a centralized staff of experts in the various fields. Could there be a better way?

I thought so in the early 1960s when I heard about the Scandinavian ombudsmen and paid them a visit in Stockholm and in Copenhagen. The ombudsman is a public official whose doors are open for redress of grievances to the humblest citizen. Ombudsmen have the power to question any government official and to examine any document. They can compel a wrong to be righted and can recommend improvements to the parliament, if they feel that the underlying law is unjust.

Because I believed that the ombudsman device might well be adapted to American needs, in 1964 I drew up a bill to establish within Congress an administrative counsel to review the case of any person who believes "that he has been denied any right or benefit to which he is entitled." Like the Congressional Research Service established in 1946, the administrative counsel was authorized to deal only with cases referred to by a member Congress, and the office was required to report its findings and recommendations only to that member.

This preserves the member's role as agent of a complaining constituent. Members could refer a case to the counsel if they wished, take credit for the result if it was favorable, and pursue the matter on their own if the counsel failed.

In an article in the *New York Times Magazine* of September 13, 1964, I set forth the case for the administrative counsel.

The main advantage would be to free legislators and their staffs from a major part of the time-consuming effort now devoted to constituents' problems. . . . Every hour saved from wrangling with the Veterans' Administration or the Social Security Administration is one that could be used for the fundamental job—researching, studying, and debating legislation. . . .

Secondly, I believe the Administrative Counsel could secure better representation for the citizen than he now obtains. The staffs of individual members are not large enough to include an expert in each of the many administrative fields with which a congressman must deal. More knowledgeable handling by a specialist could easily improve the citizen's chances for remedial action.

Third, the Administrative Counsel could avoid considerable duplication and cross-hauling. As it is now, an energetic constituent may lodge his complaint with both senators and a congressman, each of whom may conduct an investigation. The existence of the Counsel's office would mitigate this.

Fourth, the Counsel could draw general conclusions from citizens' complaints. . . . While they are spread among 535 offices, burdensome laws frequently go uncorrected, and consistently rude or lazy government officials remain undetected.

And finally, I believe the Counsel could do a better job for less money. The personal staffs of members are steadily increasing in both size and cost.[1]

Unfortunately, the proposal for a congressional ombudsman has never been acted upon. Members of Congress have been suspicious of anything they think might impair the vote-getting appeal of constituent service. Yet it is the constituent who loses through lack of an administrative counsel— in weaker services, at greater cost, and in representatives whose concentration on their primary task of legislative policy is distracted.

12

Our Constitutional System

Thomas Jefferson called the document adopted in Philadelphia on September 17, 1787, "the wisest ever yet presented." In an 1816 letter he added that each generation "has a right to choose for itself the form of government it believes most promotive of its own happiness."

Our Constitution has served us well. Its separation of powers into president, legislature, and judiciary; its federal system; and its flexibility through interpretation or amendment have made it truly the new order of the ages. Nevertheless, with Jefferson's dictum in mind, I was always alert for elements of our constitutional structure that might profit from improvement.

FEDERALISM

No agreement has been reached on the proper division of responsibility among federal, state, and local governments. Local governments, the orphans of the federal system, are frequently inequitable, inefficient, unresponsive, and nonaccountable. Under the Tenth Amendment local government is left "to the States respectively, or to the people." But a system of local government suitable for the yeomen, mechanics, and merchants of 1787, when Boston and Philadelphia were our only cities of twenty-five thousand inhabitants, is not working well today.

Federal and state governments have not solved the problem of fiscal equity, particularly in suburb-surrounded central cities, and particularly when those cities overlap state lines. Nor have they solved the problem of efficiency, with our overlapping levels of county, city, village, town, and special district. Nor of accountability, with the buck-passing possibilities of many-tiered governments with concurrent powers. Nor of responsiveness, with our unwieldy megacities that are the very antithesis of Jefferson's "ward republics." One mechanism that may offer a solution to the problem of federalism is the proposal by Ben Read and me, described in Chapter 9, for a decennial convocation of federal, state, and local representatives to make recommendations for improving federalism at all levels.

CAMPAIGN EXPENDITURES

A second area where our Constitution, as presently interpreted, may be inadequate is campaign expenditures. There the devil in the flesh is the 1976 Supreme Court decision in *Buckley v. Valeo,* holding that Congress may not validly place any limits whatever on what candidates may spend in a political campaign. Without such limits, campaign finance reform is an illusion. On November 5, 1985, I testified before the Senate Committee on Rules and Administration about my belief that *Buckley* must be interpreted away, overruled, or even nullified by a constitutional amendment if a healthy democracy is to survive:

I suggest that the Court [in *Buckley*] mistook freedom of money for freedom of speech. By barring any ceiling on overall campaign spending, it created a situation in which fund-raising has become the major preoccupation of members. . . . Both parties spend far more time raising money than they do considering ideas or policy. And the *Buckley* decision virtually guarantees that these spiraling expenditures will continue to grow.

Surely one reason why Congress is demonstrating an inability to deal with major problems is the mortgage placed on members by excessive campaign contributions.

You may well ask: why didn't the tax-writing committee undertake revision of our tax system twenty years ago? Why is it that the agriculture committees, despite floods of tears, do so little for the family farmer and so much for the corporate farm? Why aren't the banking committees in the forefront of reform legislation, rather than waiting for the initiatives of the lobbyists? . . .

The special interests will be heard to say "these contributions only buy access." But there's a gnawing fear that they involve more than access. They can influence members to adopt a friendlier view toward certain interests, or not go out of the way to antagonize them. . . . Access is a precious thing that shouldn't be for sale. . . .

So I continue to hope that one day the Supreme Court will see fit to overrule or "distinguish" the *Buckley* case, and permit Congress to impose reasonable limits on campaign expenditures. In our last months in the House in 1982, former Representatives Jonathan Bingham of New York, Millicent Fenwick of New Jersey, and I introduced a constitutional amendment to do just that.

Short of overturning the *Buckley* case's prohibition on limiting campaign expenditures, either by overruling it or by constitutional amendment, the two parties can end the hypocrisy of blaming each other for the failure to enact campaign-financing reform. Each party can adopt rules limiting its candidates' expenditures in campaigns for national office, provided the other party will do the same. Such a gambit would get around the *Buckley* case, which applies only to limits imposed by statute, not by party rule.

Can one party be shamed by public opinion into making the offer, and the other shamed into accepting it? Time will tell.

I suggest to those House Democrats who sincerely champion campaign expenditure reform: why not repeat the story of 1961, when the Democratic Study Group (see Chapter 8) spurred the House Democrats into adopting a rule enlarging the House Rules Committee and thus ending its power to block progressive legislation? Why not now get behind a proposed House rule setting limitations on what may be spent in an election campaign for a House seat? For once, the public would have a chance to see how their representatives vote.

DIVIDED GOVERNMENT

A third problem in our constitutional system lies in our separation of powers and in our often divided government.

Divided government means the presidency in the hands of one party and Congress (or at least one body of Congress) in the hands of the other. As an American way of life it started way back in 1954, when I was first elected to the House. Eisenhower, a Republican who had enjoyed a two-House Republican Congress in his first two years, now found himself confronted with a Congress controlled by the opposition.

Since 1954 divided government has reigned for thirty of forty-four years — six of Eisenhower's eight, all of Nixon's and Ford's, all of Bush's and Reagan's, and four of Clinton's eight. Leaving aside the eight years of Democratic unified government under Kennedy and Johnson, and starting with Nixon in 1969, the government has been split about four years out of five.

By the 1980s a number of us were worried. Divided government seemed to lead to deadlocks that threatened our ability to govern. Foremost was the inability of government to control skyrocketing budget deficits and the consequent increase in the national debt. Republicans wanted to get the deficit under control by cutting social spending, Democrats by raising taxes, and the result was stalemate (at least until Clinton's first two years, when a unified Democratic government managed to raise taxes and partially staunch the deficit). Nor was the deadlock in foreign policy any more edifying: in Nicaragua the Republican executive backed the contras, the Democratic majority in Congress backed the Sandinista government, and the carnage continued.

Thus in 1981 we formed the Committee on the Constitutional System. According to our prospectus, we were "a non-partisan, non-profit organization devoted to the study and analysis of the American constitutional system." The committee was chaired by Sen. Nancy Landon Kassebaum, Republican of Kansas; former treasury secretary C. Douglas Dillon;

and Lloyd N. Cutler, former presidential counsel. The members included about fifty former senators and representatives (such as William Fulbright, Richard Bolling, John Rhodes, and me), former cabinet members (such as Robert McNamara and William T. Coleman, Jr.), officials of national and state political parties, governors (such as Florida's LeRoy Collins and Virginia's Linwood Holton), university professors (such as Alexander Heard of Vanderbilt and Gerhard Casper of Stanford), journalists, lawyers, historians, political scientists (such as Norman Ornstein and James MacGregor Burns), and labor and business leaders.

The Committee on the Constitutional System met for five years, hearing witnesses and deliberating. In 1987 the bicentennial of our Constitution, the committee issued its report and recommendations.

The committee generally agreed on what had gone wrong with our constitutional system of government.

The government system provided by the Founders, we observed, separated the executive, legislative, and judicial branches and sought to prevent tyranny by checks and balances. The president could veto acts of Congress. Congress could check the president by overriding his vetoes, denying appropriations, investigating executive actions, and, in extreme cases, by impeachment. The judiciary could declare laws unconstitutional; in turn, it was subject to the power of appointment by the president and confirmation by the Senate.

That this admirable system could also produce divided government and gridlock was masked for nearly two hundred years by the early emergence of strong political parties. With their help an incoming president enjoyed a Congress of his own political party in all but four cases—1848, 1876, 1880, and 1884. And although the president occasionally lost his Congress at the midterm election, unified government regularly recurred two years later. Altogether, the United States suffered divided government only 25 percent of the time until 1950.

Undivided government accounts for the unruffled conservatism of Republican administrations from the Civil War to 1900, the whiff of Republican populism under Theodore Roosevelt, the modest activism of Democrats in Woodrow Wilson's first term, and the triumph of Republican conservatism in the 1920s and of New Deal liberalism in the 1930s and 1940s.

But the parties, in the committee's view, were weakened over the years by a number of factors. Some "good government" reforms, such as supplanting the spoils system with civil service and the basket of food from the party machine with publicly financed welfare, weakened the parties directly. Other reforms did their weakening indirectly, such as "democratizing" the nomination of congressional candidates by substituting the open primary for a primary restricted to party adherents and by substituting the presidential primaries now installed in a majority of states for the decision of party leaders or caucuses.

Another factor making for weakened parties was the enormous cost of campaigning, brought on in large part by television. This inflation of political spending coincided with the unfortunate 1976 Supreme Court decision in *Buckley v. Valeo,* that Congress was powerless to impose limits on campaign spending. To do so, the Court held, would infringe on freedom of speech. As a result, political success generally means being a multi-millionaire yourself or spending your time and losing your soul soliciting campaign funds, not from meager party treasuries but from lush special-interest contributors.

A third weakener of the party has been the American love affair with ticket splitting. Once a rare exception, ticket splitting—a proud "I vote for the person, not the party"—has become almost the norm.

All these party-weakening factors, we concluded, helped create the era of divided government. This in turn fostered deadlock and the consequent inability of government to govern, and of the public to hold responsible those who were parties to the deadlock.

Our Constitution, we further observed, lacked an effective mechanism to resolve gridlocks between the president and Congress that occur between the fixed election dates for president every four years. The off-year elections for all of the House and one-third of the Senate are seemingly too local to serve as a deadlock breaker. To be sure, the House may at any time impeach and the Senate try a failed president for "Treason, Bribery, or other high Crimes and Misdemeanors." But that is heavy artillery. Clearly, it should not be used when the dispute is simply one over policy.

Our diagnosis was clear. But when the committee looked at the remedies for divided government and gridlock, the members were unable to agree on anything very meaningful.

To reduce the likelihood of divided government, we pointed out, a constitutional amendment could make straight-ticket voting for president and Congress compulsory. This would certainly end divided government, at least in the first two years of a presidency. But legislators, who must agree to constitutional amendments by a two-thirds majority, would not take kindly to a new system that tied their political futures to that of a presidential candidate. More, ticket splitting has become an American political tradition. So our committee wisely recognized political reality and did not recommend the mandatory straight ticket.

A second method of forestalling divided government could be achieved without amending the Constitution. Congress could simply exercise its power to control election dates by setting the date for the Senate and House elections after the presidential election, say, thirty days later. Then, proponents of the proposal argue, the voters could if they wished give the president a supportive Congress. The trouble with this argument is that, given the voters' penchant for ticket splitting, they would likely go on voting for divided government.

So divided government apparently cannot be prevented. But is there a way of neutralizing the resulting gridlock when it seriously threatens the nation's capacity to govern? The committee majority saw no such method. But a substantial minority, of which I was one, offered for consideration a constitutional amendment to resolve gridlock short of the ambiguous, interminable, and heavy-handed impeachment process:

1. Adopting four-year terms for House members and eight-year terms for Senators, with elections in presidential years.
2. Empowering the President . . . or the Congress . . . to call for a prompt election to all federal offices for new, full terms.[1]

Lengthening the terms of members of Congress would have benefits beyond facilitating the proposal for extended terms plus special elections as a means of resolving gridlock or a failed presidency. As the committee pointed out, the proposal would

lengthen and coordinate the political horizons of all incumbents. Presidents and legislators could join to enact necessary measures with the promise of longer-run benefits, without having to worry about an imminent election before the benefits were realized. With fewer elections, the aggregate cost of campaign financing should go down, and legislators would be less frequently and immediately in thrall to the interest groups on whom they depend for funds. The honeymoon for enacting a President's program would be longer. With a four-year life for each Congress, the legislative process for the budget and other measures could be made more orderly and deliberate.[2]

Requiring all members of Congress and the president to run in the special election to resolve gridlock provides some assurance that it would not be frivolously or frequently used. Indeed, the mere existence of such a mechanism might help to resolve gridlock between the branches, because both president and Congress would be reluctant to face the ordeal of a general election.

Suppose the extended terms plus special elections amendment had been embodied in our Constitution during the last half century—the era of mostly divided governments and of the two challenged presidencies–Nixon's in 1974 and Clinton's in 1998. What difference would it have made?

- In 1947 the newly elected Republicans in Congress might have been tempted to call a special election with Truman down in the polls. But under the proposed extended terms plus special elections amendment,

Congress would still have been Democratic and a special election thus not in the cards.

- In 1967 President Johnson and his Vietnam War were vastly unpopular. But Congress was Democratic, the government thus not divided, and no special election would have been demanded.

- In 1973–1974 President Nixon was in deep trouble over Watergate, and the Democratic House, following the discovery of the tapes that revealed a cover-up, was ready to impeach. Nixon then resigned, and it was said that "the system worked." But without the tapes, the system might not have worked. Use of the extended terms plus special elections amendment, had it existed, might have been serviceable for the Democratic Congress.

- In late 1982 Reagan's economics were seen to be failing, and he was down in the polls. But the Democratic Congress had gone along with Reaganomics and almost certainly would not have challenged him. Suppose, however, that the Democratic Congress had stood its ground and stymied the Reagan economic program. Either the president or Congress might then have felt strong enough to call for a special election. The extended terms plus special elections regime might then have been fairly tested.

- In 1987 President Reagan was furious at what he felt to be Speaker Jim Wright's "intrusion" into the negotiations between Nicaragua's Sandinista government and the contras for a cease-fire in the long and bloody civil war. But the president, already embarrassed by revelations of his clandestine aid to the contras, would certainly not have risked calling for an election to determine who was right.

- In 1991 President Bush, who was flush with victory in the Gulf War, might have been tempted to challenge the Democratic Congress. But Congress had supported the war, and Bush surely would not have succumbed to the temptation.

- In 1994, right before the congressional sweep by the Republicans, Clinton was weak in the polls and might have been toppled. But Congress was Democratic and so would not have called for a special election.

- In late 1995 the Republican Congress threatened to close down the government if the president refused to accept its budget. President Clinton refused, and the government was closed down. The public was outraged, and under the extended terms plus special elections amendment the president could have called for a special election, except that this was the last year of his term and the mechanism would have been unavailable.

- In October 1998, as this memoir goes to press, the Monica Lewinsky affair is preoccupying the country. Unless things change, we will be embroiled perhaps until the next century in the only remedy our Constitution provides—the impeachment process. And all this at a time when grave problems, foreign and domestic, confront us. The public, to its credit, deplores the scandal but opposes impeachment. The proposal, by making available a prompt special election for both Congress and president, would have let the people decide whether they wished to keep the president they had elected.

To sum up, the proposed amendment likely would have been useful in the Nixon matter in 1973–1974, the Reagan recession of 1982, and in the Clinton impasse of October 1998.

Two other areas of our constitutional system, the presidency and the vice presidency, also need examination.

THE CEREMONIAL PRESIDENCY

Would it make sense to create a separate "chief of state" to relieve the president of endless ceremonial distractions and to reduce the temptations of "the imperial presidency"? The case for chief of state, and why it is unlikely to come to pass, were well presented in a 1975 *Newsweek* piece by Kenneth L. Woodward and Jeff B. Copeland.

[William Howard] Taft was neither the first nor the last U.S. President to complain of the almost endless ceremonial functions that clog the Chief Executive's calendar. Calvin Coolidge warned that no President could last more than 90 days in office if he allowed himself to become "the source of inspiration for every worthwhile public movement." Both Truman and Eisenhower found that ceremonial chores left precious little time for study and taking stock. And yet ceremony is essential to the magisterial aura that surrounds the nation's highest public office, and a powerful weapon in any Chief Executive's political arsenal.

To relieve future Presidents of these onerous ceremonial duties—and, more important, to divest the office itself of its almost regal trappings—Wisconsin Congressman Henry Reuss has proposed an amendment to the Constitution that would create a separate office of "Chief of State." Nominated by the President, confirmed by both houses of Congress, and subject to impeachment for high crimes, the Chief of State would serve a four-year term at a salary equal to the President's. His—or her—major duties would be to receive ambassadors and visiting heads of state and to represent the United States at similar ceremonies abroad. In this way, Reuss argues, the President would have more time to devote to running the country. At the same time, the U.S. would be spared the risk of offending other countries when—as often happens—the President must delegate lesser officials to represent the nation at foreign ceremonial gatherings held abroad.

But the real intent of the proposed amendment, as Reuss himself admits, is to strip away much of the majesty that has accrued to the President as the symbolic head of the world's most powerful nation. "The rise of the 'Imperial Presidency' during this century has posed a serious threat to the proper functioning of the checks and balances provided in the U.S. Constitution," he argues. Separation of the roles of Chief of State and Chief Executive, he feels, would go a long way toward reducing the American tendency "to deify Presidents, to render them immune from criticism, to make them our elected kings." . . .

The proposed amendment has received mixed reviews from libertarians on both the left and right. Political philosopher Michael Novak, a former speechwriter for Democratic Presidential candidates, favors the scheme because he believes it would introduce "a powerful wedge between the President's ability to *personify* the public and to *persuade* the public of a political course of action." Such a wedge, Novak argues, would no longer allow the President to adopt "a moral stature to which his deeds did not entitle him." Conservative pundit George Will agrees, but doubts that the majesty of the Chief of State can be separated from the raw practical power that the President wields. "Alas," Will wrote recently, "Reuss is incorrect in believing that Americans will be distracted by an empty ceremonial office." . . .

Even so, Representative Reuss believes that events in recent history have proved the need to demythologize the U.S. Presidency. . . . "If a Chief of State had been around," the Wisconsin Democrat concludes, "Nixon would not have lasted very long."[3]

THE VICE PRESIDENCY

In 1986, as a member of the Twentieth Century Fund's ten-member Task Force on the Vice-Presidency, I joined professors Hugh Heclo and Arthur M. Schlesinger, Jr., in a dissenting opinion suggesting that the vice presidency be abolished:

We believe that long experience has proved the office of the vice president to be beyond redemption. The Constitution assigns no role to the vice president except to preside over the Senate, to cast a vote in case of a tie, and to succeed to the president's powers and duties in case of the death, disability, removal, or resignation of a president. Efforts have been made from time to time to invest the vice presidency with substance. These efforts have uniformly failed.

The only real point of the office is to provide for presidential succession. But far from preparing the occupant for the presidency, the frustrations inseparable from the office have made it as often a maiming as a making experience, a process of emasculation rather than of education.

The modern vice presidency that has developed with little forethought over the past thirty years is proving a more disruptive than constructive feature of our political system. First, the contemporary office both confers unfair political advantages on its holder in the contest for the presidential nomination and traps him, once nominated, into identification with policies that he may privately reject but could not, as vice president, publicly oppose—results that are bad for the incumbent party and bad for the country. Second, the recent development of a vice presidential bureaucracy with few real functions to perform and limited accountability to Congress increases the potential for mischief at the summit of government. Finally, the process of selecting vice presidential candidates in the heat of modern presidential campaigns has not worked reliably to produce qualified nominees; instead, the process has increasingly served to create a secondary personality contest in national elections.[4]

Heclo, Schlesinger, and I suggested a potential solution—a constitutional amendment abolishing the vice presidency and providing for a special election to be held ninety days after the death, disability, resignation, or removal of a president; in the interim the acting president would be a member of the cabinet according to the order set forth in the Succession Act of 1886 (secretary of state, secretary of the treasury, and so on).

Where are we left in this grand exploration of our constitutional system? Pretty much where we started. The first proposed constitutional amendment I discussed, a convocation to improve the federal system, could be more easily achieved by a simple presidential proclamation for such a convocation and a focusing of public opinion on the responsibility of federal and state legislatures to address whatever recommendations the convocation might make.

The second problem, reform of campaign expenditures, should be first addressed by attempting to distinguish or overrule *Buckley v. Valeo*, or by changes in Democratic and Republican party rules.

But for the third constitutional problem, divided government that causes gridlock, the extended terms plus special elections remedy would seem to provide a better solution for the Nixon impeachment, the Reagan recession, and the Lewinsky scandal. But who really knows?

The last two constitutional amendments I discussed—a ceremonial presidency and abolishing the vice presidency—have such slight chance of adoption that pursuing them seems not worth the trouble.

Thus I conclude that the general principle of not lightly amending the Constitution—which certainly applies to bad amendments like school prayer, abortion, flag burning, a balanced budget, supermajorities for tax increases, and term limits—should apply as well to the five structural proposals I have discussed here.

Campaigning (with Assemblyman Robert Landry) against Senator Joseph McCarthy, 1952

A backyard rally against Senator Joseph McCarthy, 1952

Discussing American cities with President Jimmy Carter, 1977

Practicing T'ai Chi in Tiananmen Square, 1977 (File photograph. Copyright © 1998 Journal Sentinel Inc., reproduced with permission.)

The Joint Economic Committee (Senator Paul Sarbanes of Maryland, Representative Parren Mitchell of Maryland, Senator Edward Kennedy of Massachusetts, Representative Margaret Heckler of Massachusetts), 1981 (Photograph by Azar Hammond)

Appearing with Representative Millicent Fenwick of New Jersey on "Meet the Press," 1982 (Photograph by Reni Newsphotos, Inc.)

Studying questionnaire responses

Wisconsin colleagues Clement Zablocki and David Obey wish me well in retirement, 1983

congressman

HENRY S. REUSS

January, 1981

Reagan's First 100 Days

Ronald Reagan's inaugural on January 20 has a lot in common with that of Franklin D. Roosevelt back in 1933. FDR had decisively beaten the Republican incumbent, Herbert Hoover. He achieved this simply by promising a new face and a new can-do spirit. To the extent that his platform got specific—as in his pledge to cut the budget—nobody paid much attention, and the pledge was soon discarded.

FDR then used the first 100 days of his presidency to establish that the United States was not going to splinter into hundreds of selfish groups, but instead could govern itself. The first 100 days worked. With Congress' help, FDR

reopened the banks, created jobs, provided relief for the destitute, salvaged home mortgages, guaranteed labor the right to bargain and to a minimum wage. All this action convinced most Americans that "the only thing we have to fear is fear itself".

Now, 48 years later, President Reagan faces his first 100 days. He defeated overwhelmingly President Carter, because the people associated the hapless

Franklin D. Roosevelt

incumbent with a misery-laden inflation, intolerably high interest rates, and economic stagnation.

In 1980, as in 1932, the people voted for change and action —"Don't just stand there, do something"—though they weren't quite clear what the action ought to be. People in 1932 weren't really sure that FDR's proclaimed fiscal conservatism was the way out, but FDR promised action, and that was enough.

Similarly, I suspect that Americans in 1980 voted for a change. To the extent that Governor Reagan's campaign program grew specific—to fight inflation by increasing the

deficit through a massive individual tax cut, and through heavier military spending—many of us wondered why this wouldn't simply make inflation and interest rates even worse. But Governor Reagan did promise a change, and that was enough.

Now the question is: Will President Reagan in his first 100 days do what FDR did—rally the nation to get a grip on our economic destiny? And here, what is important to look at is not what Governor Reagan said in the campaign, but what he does in his first 100 days.

The only program that will work is one that the American people perceive as being genuinely aimed at inflation and stagnation. A Republican program aimed at shifting real income from the middle class to those at the top of the income scale would be just as irrelevant to this purpose as a Democratic program continuing past Democratic economic errors. Happily, there is a way out, a program that most Americans would welcome: (1) Get the budget and inflation under control, by believable methods. (2) Bring down interest rates as the best way of encouraging capital investment. (3) Simplify and streamline government at all levels.

Ronald Reagan

I'll be very much involved in this question of where we go economically because I've decided to take the chairmanship, for the new 97th Congress, of the Joint Economic Committee. With the Republicans in control of the Senate, and the Democrats of the House, the Joint Committee offers a real chance to work out a bipartisan policy, and at the very least to provide a forum for each side to state its views. With luck, we can avoid both old Democratic mistakes and new Republican mistakes. It is a challenge and an opportunity.

Cover page from a Reuss newsletter

'Are you suggesting we pay taxes kinda like common, ordinary folk?'

Bill Sanders cartoon (File cartoon. Copyright © 1998 Journal Sentinel Inc.,
reproduced with permission.)

Part III

TAPERING OFF
(1983 and After)

13

Discovering Nongovernmental Organizations

My decision to retire from Congress at the end of 1982 was not a difficult one. Congress had become much less collegial and more contentious. Costs of campaigning were escalating, and the time and bootlicking necessary to raise funds were becoming insupportable.

Then, too, my personal position argued for moving on. I had given up my post as chairman of the banking committee because its work was increasingly bound up with unattractive minutiae, and because I wanted to head the Joint Economic Committee during the first years of Reaganomics. Now the JEC had fought its battle; under the rules the chairmanship would pass to the Senate in 1983 for two years, and I would be bereft of the chairman's powers I had enjoyed. All told, at age seventy, it was time to move on.

But to what? I had made no plans at all for retirement. Soon opportunities appeared—in teaching, business, and the law. The one I picked was a bipolar law practice—senior partner in the large Washington firm of Chapman Duff and Paul, founded by Oscar Chapman, Truman's secretary of the interior, and serving as "counsel" for the energetic young Milwaukee firm of Charne and Tehan. For three years I divided my time between the two, avoiding lobbying and concentrating on such civil matters as immigration, the environment, wills and estates, and venture investments.

By 1986 I began to ask myself: why am I doing this? My legal associates were stimulating and friendly, but the subject matter, after the excitement of Congress, was uninspiring. Besides, couldn't nongovernmental organizations at least partly leaven the lump that the Reagan administration was making of my beloved country? I decided to explore the possibilities.

First on the list were the housing organizations. This was a subject that had absorbed me from my first dabbling in Milwaukee housing fifty years earlier through my chairmanship of the House Committee on Banking, Finance, and Urban Affairs and of its Subcommittee on the City.

In 1983 James Rouse, the brilliant Baltimore developer of shopping malls and festival marketplaces, was then seventy and had decided to retire and place his wealth and his wisdom at the service of his newly formed Enterprise Foundation. Jim and his wife, Patty, asked me to become one of the foundation's first trustees. I jumped at the chance and have served on the board ever since.

The foundation's mission is "to see that all low-income people in America have fit and affordable housing and the chance to move up and out of poverty into the mainstream of American life." Some thought this hopelessly ambitious, but Jim's motto was "What ought to be, can be, when you have the will to make it so." Enterprise, operating through about seven hundred neighborhood nonprofits, has disbursed roughly $2.1 billion and produced more than seventy-two thousand new and renovated homes.

Early on, we learned that decent housing alone cannot bring about genuine transformation. Community development must be holistic, with attention not just to homes but to jobs, public safety, schools, health, and child care. To this end, Enterprise has concentrated its efforts in sixteen cities in ways designed to achieve this "critical mass" effect.

One such place is Sandtown-Winchester, a square-mile area near downtown Baltimore. A few years ago this was a drug-infested, poverty-stricken, hopeless no-man's-land. Today, because of Enterprise's "total community" approach, Sandtown-Winchester has come alive again, with new and refurbished homes, reformed schools, community policing, a restored food market, and neighborhood government—Thomas Jefferson's ward republic coming true.

Jim Rouse died in April 1996, but his good work is continued by Patty and by Bart Harvey, his successor as chairman. Its activities are paralleled by two other exemplary housing organizations—the Local Initiatives Support Corporation and the church-related Habitat for Humanity. But all three work in harmony and demonstrate that the private sector is not wholly powerless to address the gap caused by government downsizing. I dream that the prospect of creating scores of urban transformations around the country might inspire one of America's new billionaires to do for our inner cities what Ted Turner did for the UN and George Soros for Russia.

I had a number of other postcongressional opportunities in low-income housing. When Wisconsin essentially dissolved its low-income housing program in the early 1980s—mistakenly, in my view—it formed a nonprofit called the Wisconsin Housing Partnership, of which I became the first president. Because it has been operating on a shoestring budget, its production has been unimpressive.

A related activity was Wisconsin's energy program for low-income families. The Wisconsin Gas Light Company realized that it could not simply turn off the heat on an impoverished family during the winter cold. So it organized a task force, headed by Republican state senator "Tiny" Krueger and me, to devise a program of utility regulation and state aid that would prevent such tragedies. Tiny, whose enormous girth could be guessed from his nickname, was a delight to work with.

As the 1990s approached, a major threat to much of the nation's stock of assisted housing appeared on the horizon. Federal programs in the 1970s had encouraged developers to construct low- and moderate-income apartments. The hitch was that the subsidies would run out in fifteen years, when the operators would be free to throw out their tenants and rent the apartments to the highest bidders. Was there a way to prevent this looming catastrophe? The Ford Foundation set up a task force to find out, headed by Carla Hills, the former Republican secretary of housing and urban development, and me. We found it easy to work together. Our recommendation, essentially to preserve the assisted character of the apartments with the lowest subsidy possible, was adopted by Congress. At least, the worst was avoided.

There followed another task force on which I served, set up by the National Farm Housing Association and chaired by my old friend Cushing Dolbeare. We brought about some needed reforms in the farm housing program that dated to the 1930s.

Economics also remained high on my list of retirement priorities. John Wright, an economist who found it more satisfying to operate his investment advisory firm in depressed Bridgeport, Connecticut, than on glamorous Wall Street, set up the Committee on Developing American Capitalism. I was on his board, along with a number of economists I admired, including James Tobin of Yale, Benjamin Friedman of Harvard, and Walter Hoadley of the Bank of America. Its publications included my "How to Make a Million Jobs" (see the notes for Chapter 6).

Still another interest was foreign policy. I became vice chair of the Association to Unite the Democracies, chaired by my old congressional Republican friend Henry Smith of Buffalo. This organization was a direct descendant of the Union Now movement, established by journalist Clarence Streit right after World War II to try to prevent the demoralization and decay of the democracies that occurred during the Hitler days. At the association I worked on a new form of post–cold war political and economic organization. These efforts got a boost when I ran into my old friend, recently retired ambassador John W. Tuthill. I had known Jack in my congressional travels. When Jack was the U.S. delegate to the Organization for Economic Cooperation and Development, he had helped me to study that energetic outfit at its Paris headquarters for several weeks. And when he was our ambassador to Brazil during the bad days of the military junta, he quietly put me in touch with some democratic-minded dissidents in Rio whose insights proved helpful. Jack and I produced the proposal for a Concert of the Democracies (see Chapter 4).

I got another peek into foreign policy in 1992, at the behest of my son, Mike, who had become a hot public interest lawyer in Portland, Oregon. He and a half-dozen other Oregon lawyers were headed to Miami to assist the thousands of refugees from the military dictatorship in Haiti. The refugees could avoid deportation if they could prove they were political refugees, in fear for their lives, rather than simply economic refugees. I came aboard the little mission as an octogenarian hitchhiker. We all worked hard for several weeks at the Haitian Relief Agency, helping these Creole-speaking have-nots to get their immigration papers properly filled out.

Shortly after Clinton's election, it became apparent that Florida could not be the haven for the countless Haitians who wished to emigrate. A better way would be to undo the military coup in Haiti and restore the lawfully elected government of President Jean-Bertrand Aristide, in exile in Washington. To his credit, after some wobbling and in the face of the CIA's slanderous onslaught on Aristide, Clinton, aided by Jimmy Carter, Gen. Colin Powell, and Sen. Sam Nunn of Georgia, ousted the dictatorship and restored Aristide. I continued my interest in Haiti, organizing a bipartisan group of former members of Congress to monitor the progress of reconstruction on the island.

I made another venture south of the border in 1997 when I became a director of the Magrath Foundation, named in honor of Margaret's father, an Alberta energy pioneer. The foundation's mission is to develop community-based energy projects that help needy people and protect the environment. Its current model is aiding Nicaraguans living in the largest undisturbed rain forest in North America, to better their hard lot. Although they once fought each other in the civil war between Sandinistas and contras, they now work together. They are desperately poor, lacking electricity, potable water, and any agricultural opportunity beyond slash-and-burn. With firewood their only source of energy, they threaten their forest home. In 1987 a young American engineer, Ben Linder, was murdered by a band of contra guerrillas as he labored on a hydroelectric project on a forest stream. His vision, carried on by other volunteers, has now produced two working hydro projects. Each supplies communities of about five thousand inhabitants with safe drinking water and with electricity for household use that saves the need to cut firewood, lights the health clinic, and powers a machine shop and a rice-drying facility. The native cooperatives that operate the electricity generators sponsor benign agricultural methods (rather than slash-and-burn) to save the remaining rain forest and reforestation to restore denuded areas. The rain forest protects precious varieties of plants and animals, furnishes a winter habitat for many of our migrating songbirds, and by absorbing carbon dioxide counters global warming. The Nicaraguan venture combines renewable and nonpolluting energy, help for some poor North Americans devastated by a decade of civil war abetted by our government, and steps to save a precious rain forest.

I also profited much from my work with the Washington Institute for Foreign Affairs, an organization of former diplomats, legislators, and military officials. As a director, I helped line up the frequent excellent speakers who kept our membership current.

Two other nongovernmental organizations on which I served as director were the Committee on the Constitutional System, described in Chapter 12, and Common Cause, which concerns itself with campaign financing reform.

Other activities were closer to Wisconsin. One related to my long interest in preserving Wisconsin's glacial geology so that these unique earth forms continue to give joy to hikers, campers, and nature lovers generally. I had sponsored the legislation setting up the Ice Age National Scientific Reserve and the Ice Age National Scenic Trail. The trail will one day traverse one thousand miles, from Sturgeon Bay to the Minnesota border. But only about 225 miles of the trail have been officially certified to date, so its supporters still have miles to go before they sleep. I have continued my interest in the trail, contributing sweat, money, and ideas to keep it moving forward. Its adherents, working through the Ice Age Foundation, are an inspiring group of outdoorspeople.

A vital section of southeastern Wisconsin's glacial moraines lies in Washington and Waukesha Counties, one of the last great areas basically unprotected from development and quarrying. With Ody Fish, former state Republican Party chair, I led a 1996 task force of the Wisconsin Academy of Arts, Sciences and Letters, which produced a proposal to save the Kettle Moraine by a combination of public and private effort (see Chapter 5). As I write, the state Department of Natural Resources and the legislature have endorsed the proposal, and it looks as if the Kettle Moraine may yet be rescued.

The 1996 Kettle Moraine report of the Wisconsin Academy's task force led to a second report, in September 1998, "Discouraging Urban Sprawl and Encouraging Compact Development." Noting that southeastern Wisconsin's uncontrolled development "intensifies highway congestion and air pollution, burdens taxpayers with the expense of building isolated schools, firehouses, police stations, road and utilities," we recommended that voters needle their local governments to follow the existing sound regional anti-sprawl land-use plan. This plan would concentrate new development so as to save what is left of nature's beauty. Our report cited Portland, Oregon, as a worthy model of smart growth.

Another Wisconsin interest arose from the wave of restorations of historic buildings that took place in the 1980s, much of it through tax subsidies obtained through the leadership of the National Trust for Historic Preservation. As my congressional days were ending, I formed several partnerships to save such nineteenth-century historic Milwaukee buildings as Knapp-Astor House, a charming Queen Anne dwelling, and the German-English Academy on Broadway, a Late-Picturesque school structure. Both were saved from the wrecker's ball and became successful small office buildings. A third venture, also on Broadway, was the fortress-like abandoned Blatz Brewery. This I tried to convert into moderately priced rental cooperatives, but the co-op approach was unfamiliar to Milwaukeeans, and I was lucky to be able to turn the project over to a Minneapolis developer who has successfully converted it to rental apartments.

Historic rehabilitation must have been much on the minds of both Reusses during the 1980s. In 1980 our daughter Jackie, now living in France, showed us a wondrous ruined tower on the River Lot in southwestern France near Cahors. Still standing were only the four thick limestone walls. Its last owner, known locally as "The Tonkinese," had gone off to fight in Indochina in the 1870s and had never returned. A fig tree was growing out of the foundation, and a limpid spring occupied what had been the ground floor. The village, which had long since fallen heir to the relic, quickly arranged a sale. The rehabilitation process began, with its endless parleys with local masons, plumbers, carpenters, and electricians, and with the departmental office of historic buildings. Margaret's superb capabilities as general contractor enabled the repairs to be finished surprisingly quickly. We have been spending our summers there ever since, exploring the painted caves, Roman villas, medieval fortifications, and ancient villages. We became so enchanted that in 1993 we wrote *The Unknown South of France: A Travel Buff's Guide.*

I have found two new hobbies, mycology and lepidoptery. In France and in Wisconsin morels, sulfur polyphores, and puffballs and swallowtails, admirals, commas, and painted ladies have entered my life. Mushrooms and butterflies have been added to my long fascination with birds, rocks, trees, flowers, and all living things.

Another blessing of retirement was that I finally found some time to read. Rejecting channel surfing and Internet chatting, I reintroduced myself to Thackeray's *Henry Esmond* and *Vanity Fair,* Balzac's *Père Goriot,* Dickens's *David Copperfield,* Mann's *The Story of a Cheat,* Roth's *Radetzky March,* Mark Twain's *Connecticut Yankee,* Santayana's *The Last Puritan,* Montaigne's *Essays,* Macaulay's *History of England,* lots of Trollope, Colette, William Trevor, Patrick Lee Fermor, and Robertson Davies, Plato's *Republic,* the Bible, plays of Ibsen, Shakespeare, Shaw, O'Neill, Goethe, Pagnol, Giraudoux, Dürrenmatt, and Rostand, and the poetry of Villon, Ovid, Browning, Emily Dickinson, Whitman, Eliot.

I have continued to enjoy good health, through the surgical and pharmaceutical breakthroughs of the National Institutes of Health (NIH) and through the excellent care of two health maintenance organizations, George Washington University and Kaiser Permanente. The latter is convenient to our salubrious present home on San Francisco Bay, to which we retired in 1995. My support in Congress of the NIH and the HMO turn out to have a few benefits for me in my old age.

In far-off places I've even flirted with alternative medicine. In Bavaria and the French Alps I enjoyed the healing waters of the thermal spas. In China I practiced T'ai Chi in Tiananmen Square and underwent acupuncture by barefoot doctors in the countryside. And in the Yucatán Club Med I had a near-perfect attendance record at yoga classes.

Retirement also brought a new domestic assignment: cook. Though my repertoire remains limited, I produce a creditable cassoulet with beans and duck, lamb patty with sour cream and capers, and grilled tuna with salsa.

14

Reflections on the Golden Age

Looking back, I take pride in the achievements of the two decades from roughly 1948 to 1968, a golden age when government was good. The values of government then seemed the old values of three earlier golden ages in our national history: that of the Founders, Washington and Franklin and Jefferson, the Declaration of Independence, Constitution, and Bill of Rights; that of Lincoln—the Gettysburg Address and the struggle against slavery and for the union; and that of FDR—the New Deal and the Four Freedoms, and the fight against depression and the dictators.

Those old values as they developed were, and are, freedom—of speech, religion, assembly, the person, and from want and fear; equality—of opportunity and with the promise that existing inequalities of income and wealth would not be worsened; fraternity—a society based on community and cooperation rather than on class; justice—the rule of law and a sense of fairness; honor—the Golden Rule in public as in private life.[1] Where they conflict, it is the task of statesmanship to resolve the conflict.

The prelude to our golden age of 1948–1968 was FDR's New Deal and World War II. Though some of FDR's reforms—banking, farm policy, regulation of transportation and communication—may seem passé today, the solid body of Social Security, unemployment compensation, protection for investors, minimum wages, and school lunches lives on. And never has a nation marshaled its resources more effectively than America did in World War II.

But the great questions as the postwar years began were whether the governments to follow could continue the equalizing thrust of the New Deal, whether they could achieve full employment in peacetime and basic civil rights for African Americans (two goals the New Deal had failed to achieve), and whether they could lay the foundation for preventing a nuclear World War III.

Between the late 1940s and the late 1960s government proved that it could.

Harry Truman brought the Employment Act, integration in the military, the United Nations, the Marshall Plan, his Point Four program for helping poor countries, and NATO.

From Ike came an era of good feeling that did not seek to dismantle the gains already made.

From JFK came the Peace Corps, support for European unity, the Alliance for Progress, a cool head in the 1962 Cuban nuclear crisis, a stand for human rights, and an effort to educate the people for big things to come.

From LBJ, full employment without inflation, civil rights, the War on Poverty, Medicare, support for the environment, cities, and education—all clouded by Vietnam.

From Congress, civility, internal reform, elections relatively unbought, and a willingness despite the cold war to end the witch hunts and disband the House Un-American Activities Committee. The sins of Congress, such as a tendency to overlegislate and to overhype its achievements, were venial.

From the Supreme Court, a ringing defense of freedom, ranging from school desegregation to one person, one vote to fairer criminal procedures.

Somewhat later but still attributable to the golden age of 1948–1968 and its basic values were such achievements of the 1970s as Neighborhood Advisory Councils, Community Reinvestment, the Consumer Cooperative Bank, the opening to China, the Camp David accords, Clean Air and Clean Water Acts, and voting rights for eighteen-year-olds.

After 1968 came hard times for the government. Dislocations from the Vietnam War and the two OPEC price increases brought on the stagflation of the 1970s.

Reaganomics followed in the 1980s—a reckless increase in the national debt; huge tax cuts for the wealthy; "immense expense, mainly for defense" (as the Capital Steps singers put it); a lurch toward greater economic inequality.

With it came a decline in the virtues that characterized the eras of good government. *Freedom?* The Supreme Court held that freedom to spend unlimited amounts to gain public office outranked the freedom of government to remain unbought. *Equality?* The gap in incomes and wealth between the lower two-thirds of our people and the upper one-third was steadily widening. *Fraternity?* Government was encouraging the haves to conclude that they were no longer their brothers' keepers. *Justice?* We seemed to be recalling Anatole France's taunt that the rich and the poor both have the right to sleep under bridges. *Honor?* Scandals, real and contrived, trickled out of Washington daily.

Small wonder that many Americans, looking at their society, felt as did W. B. Yeats that "the best lack all conviction, while the worst are full of passionate intensity."

This waning of the golden age when government was good, I believe, had two main causes.

First was the increasing militarization of American society. Eisenhower at least balanced his armed foray into Lebanon and our subversions in Iran and Guatemala with a farewell warning against the rising "military-industrial complex." His sins were as nothing compared with the destructiveness and mendacity of the Vietnam War under LBJ and Nixon.

There followed the generation-long expansion of cold war military spending; our orgy of arms shipments and military training for the developing world; and a series of military interventions in Grenada, Lebanon, Nicaragua, and elsewhere.

Always we suffered runaway CIA "covert actions" like its 1953 coup restoring Iran's ousted shah, its 1954 coup in favor of a military dictatorship against the legitimate government in Guatemala, its 1961 Bay of Pigs invasion, its thirty-year sponsorship of the larcenous Mobutu in Zaire.

Although the cold war is over, the "peace dividend" still eludes us. Our annual military spending of about a quarter-trillion dollars is greater than the military spending of all the other powers combined.

With guns on the brain, the government began to forget our heritage of freedom, equality, fraternity, justice, and honor. After attending a prayer breakfast devoted to the Judeo-Christian ideal of peace on earth, public servants spent the rest of the day encouraging the new militarism.

The second major cause of the waning of the golden age was the increase in inequality from the 1970s on. For forty years equality in our society, both in human rights directly and in terms of income and wealth, had been increasing, with the lower two-thirds of American families improving their lot at the expense of a slight decrease in the share of the top one-third. But by the 1970s this trend had begun to reverse itself, in large part because of the stagflation that was becoming endemic (see Chapter 6).

This increase in inequality through stagflation was greatly accentuated under Reaganomics. Inaugurating a deliberate policy of providing goodies for the wealthy, Reaganomics combined large income tax cuts for the wealthiest 20 percent of Americans with large increases in the Social Security tax levies on workers; hostility to the unions by breaking up the air traffic controllers' strike; slashes in federal programs for the poor and the middle class; and a generally easy-going attitude toward swollen executive compensation and speculative corporate takeovers.

Just as the militarization of America in the last thirty years has made the old virtues less appealing to the public, so growing inequality has created a large new class, perhaps a fifth of our people, who look upon their enlarged incomes and wealth as something bestowed by heaven and hence not to be shared, in the interest of a cohesive society, with those below. From their freeways, suburban shopping malls, and gated communities the wealthy easily blame minorities, single mothers, immigrants, and others for their plight—anything but the automation or the globalization or the Reagan reshuffling or the fetish of the completely free market, all of which are much more probable causes.

While the years since 1968 have not been exactly America's dark ages, they have surely been less than golden. It might have been otherwise. Suppose that Robert Kennedy had not been cut down by an assassin's bullet in June 1968. With Kennedy spared, and with Gene McCarthy's throwing his support to him at the Chicago convention, Bobby could have secured the nomination and won the election, albeit narrowly. Had he served for two terms, he could have ended the Vietnam War in 1969 rather than six years later; limited the inflationary damage of the first oil price shock by rationing gasoline; and avoided both the price controls and the loose money of the early seventies. And with peace and a growing economy, he could have put a real dent in poverty and inequality. Suppose further that with Kennedy's blessing Mo Udall had succeeded him as president for two terms, beginning in 1976. Udall could have ended the cold war in 1979 rather than ten years later—by agreeing to help the Russians reconstruct their society and economy in return for their dissolution of communism and their empire. He could have avoided the heavy-handed money tightening, tax cutting, military spending, and poor-people bashing of the Reagan years. If the reader objects that this fantasy hands the Democrats sixteen of the thirty-two presidential years from 1969 to the year 2000, I will gladly cede the second sixteen years of this fantasy—1984 to 2000—to true Republican conservatives, of the stripe of Lincoln, Teddy Roosevelt, Wendell Willkie, and Eisenhower, under whom the golden years could have rolled on quite nicely.

Fantasies aside, what are the chances of recapturing in the twenty-first century the social contract that reigned in the middle years of the twentieth?

Our country has a good record of working its way out of the doldrums. It can again. The Republican Party will have to go back to the governmental responsibility of Lincoln, Teddy Roosevelt, and Eisenhower, unlikely though it be. My party, the Democrats, will have to repeat what the Democratic Organizing Committee did in Wisconsin in the late 1940s and what the Democratic Study Group did in the House in the 1960s—reform itself. And the leaders of that new century reform movement must march under the banner of equality.

If there is to be a fifth golden age in the early twenty-first century, it will have to include some formula for reinvolving individuals and families in public life. In 1832 Alexis de Tocqueville in his *Democracy in America* foresaw this love for nongovernmental organizations: "Americans of all ages, all conditions and dispositions constantly favor associations . . . to give entertainments, to found seminaries, to build inns, to construct churches, to diffuse books, to send missionaries to the antipodes." What I learned about the potential for nongovernmental organization (see Chapter 13) may well be the way to do it.

Of course, what we need is leadership. But we also need followership. As I told a recent graduating class at the University of Wisconsin-Milwaukee:

The Muse of History may now be willing to grant us a second chance. In personal life, instead of a polarized choice between the society oriented and the career oriented, why not recognize that the good life partakes of both, that the idealism of Don Quixote can merge with the practicality of Sancho Panza?

A healthier view of one's own life can lead to a healthier society. Pericles was right when he told the Athenians that the citizen who takes no part in public affairs is not merely unambitious but useless. If you will combine the private aim of getting ahead in life with the public pursuit of justice, you will help restore the essence of democracy—informed and lively participation by its citizens. And that can produce a government which feels compelled neither to do everything nor to do nothing.

If you are to play your role in reviving the faith of the American people in their government, how appropriate that you today receive your degrees not from some elite academy, not from some hall where the ivy was planted long ago, but from the University of Wisconsin–Milwaukee—founded to bring higher education not just to the elite but to the sons and daughters of the common people. So you will need not just a telescope to fix on the heavens of power and success, where you hope you're headed, but a microscope, so you may look gratefully back on the plain people from whom you are sprung—people who believed in the power of good government to do good!

Notes

Index

Notes

CHAPTER 1. GROWING UP GERMAN AMERICAN

1. Needlemaker and buttonmaker are honorable antecedents and leave me with no regret that I cannot claim descent from the princely line of Henry of Reuss. The tiny principality of Reuss (Elder Line) was located in Thuringia in eastern Germany. Founded in the eleventh century, it was a member of the Holy Roman Empire and later, until its dissolution in 1920, of Germany. By custom, every male member of the princely family was named Henry, numbered up to one hundred before the numbering starting again. In 1965 I actually visited Greiz, the capital of the principality of Reuss. The communist commissars then in charge proudly showed me the winter palace, the summer palace, and the house of parliament, all now turned to other uses. And in my travels I met several Prince Henrys of Reuss, one the owner of large forests in Austria, another the representative in Bonn of Mercedes-Benz.

2. Brademas and I were much impressed by the reverent manner of addressing the presidents of the German universities: *Magnificenz* and *Spectabilus*. Brademas later became president of New York University, but no evidence exists that he demanded any similar salutation.

CHAPTER 3. THE ROCKY ROAD TO CAPITOL HILL

1. The comments are collected in my FBI file of November 1948, obtained pursuant to the Freedom of Information Act in 1980. According to a member of the Milwaukee bar, "Henry Reuss has locally provoked considerable comment because of his 'very forward social views,' but he has never . . . indicated he was sympathetic to any organization or country that embraced hostile ideas to American institutions." A partner in my law firm told the FBI: "Although I and most of the other partners in the firm differed considerably from Mr. Reuss on domestic matters, Mr. Reuss at no time ever indicated in his activities or discussions the slightest disloyalty to the U.S." A Milwaukee neighbor stated that "although she disagreed with him completely in his views on domestic matters, she has never had any occasion to doubt his patriotism"; a North Lake neighbor "considered the views of Henry Reuss to be very provocative, but . . . never . . . un-American."

CHAPTER 4. FOREIGN POLICY

1. Henry S. Reuss, "Breaking the Stalemate," *Commonweal,* June 20, 1958, pp. 295–98.

2. Henry S. Reuss, "Point Four Youth Corps," *Commonweal,* May 6, 1960, pp. 146–48.

3. Letter from Tris Coffin, February 7, 1990, Henry S. Reuss. Papers, 1839–1982. Milwaukee Manuscript Collection 112. State Historical Society of Wisconsin. These papers are held in the Golda Meir Library, the University of Wisconsin–Milwaukee.

4. Andy Young and Barbara Jordan of Texas, two splendid representatives, were elected in 1972, the first black southerners elected to the House since Reconstruction. The Voting Rights Act of 1965 had by then enfranchised large numbers of southern blacks.

5. My endorsement of Gene McCarthy in 1968 was merely the first in my many unsuccessful endorsements of candidates for the Democratic presidential nomination. In 1972 I supported Sen. Ed Muskie of Maine, because he combined opposition to the Vietnam War with leadership on issues like urban policy and the environment. He was badly beaten by Sen. George McGovern of South Dakota in the Wisconsin primary and soon withdrew.

In 1976 my candidate for the nomination was my House colleague Mo Udall of Arizona. Rep. Dave Obey of Wisconsin and I loved Mo for his integrity and wit and took the lead in suggesting that he enter the race. Cheered by Mo's early lead, we listened to the Wisconsin primary returns at headquarters at Milwaukee's Hotel Schroeder. Against cautionary pleading from me and Obey that returns from many rural precincts weren't in yet, and that those precincts might well be attracted by Carter's religious fundamentalism, Mo's advisers urged him to go downstairs to the ballroom to declare victory. He did, and the early editions of the morning papers carried pictures of a victorious Mo and a wildly cheering crowd. But when the final count came in, Carter had triumphed and went on to win the nomination and the presidency. Obey and I still believe that had Udall won, he could have restored to the nation the elan of the 1948–1968 years and thus would have changed for the better the history of the twentieth century's last quarter.

In 1980, disappointed with Carter's self-induced recession, I backed Ted Kennedy. In addition to my personal friendship with Ted, I backed him because he opposed Carter's self-made high-interest-rate recession. But the Kennedy campaign never got off the ground. Once again it was Carter's win over Kennedy in the Wisconsin primary that cinched Carter's renomination.

In 1984, for the first time in twenty years, I supported for the Democratic nomination someone who turned out to be the winning candidate. Walter Mondale, the former vice president, was an honorable and intelligent man with the courage to challenge Reaganomics' thesis that the more you lower taxes, the more revenue you create. Mondale won the nomination, was roundly defeated by Ronald Reagan, and went on to serve as a highly successful ambassador to Japan in the Clinton administration.

In 1988 I declared for Sen. Paul Simon of Illinois the day he announced his candidacy. He combined a political lifetime of fighting for worthy causes with the homespun quality of his hero Abraham Lincoln. Simon's quest for the nomination fell victim to the superior campaign organization of Massachusetts governor Mike Dukakis, who won the primary, only to lose in the general election to George Bush.

In 1992 I endorsed early on former representative and senator Paul Tsongas of Massachusetts. As a first-term representative, Paul had been a member of my Banking Committee. Campaigning for him in his native Lowell, I had seen at first hand his successful efforts to bring life back to what had been a doomed and dying mill town. Fresh from his triumph in the early New Hampshire primary, Paul now was determined to win in Maryland. I introduced him to the big crowd at his opening rally in Baltimore. He won the Maryland primary but shortly was swamped by Bill Clinton's string of southern victories. My unimpressive record of candidate selection had suffered one more blow.

6. In the campaign Agnew committed the ethnic slur of calling Polish Americans *Polacks*. Concerned by the threat to their share of the Polish American vote, GOP leaders asked their popular Polish American House member, Edward Derwinski of Illinois, to try to rescue Agnew. Eddie obliged, pointing out that Shakespeare, a man as free of bigotry as they come, had Horatio say of Hamlet's father (*Hamlet*, act 1, scene 1):

> So frown'd he once, when, in an angry parle,
> He smote the sledded Polacks on the ice.

Something had to be done to neutralize Eddie's attempt to rehabilitate Agnew, and I was asked to counterpunch. Fortunately, I remembered that a rural Wisconsin scholar, Charles D. Stewart, known as the Sage of Pike Lake, held that what Shakespeare had *really* said was:

> He smote his leaded pole-axe on the ice.

So I quickly made public this version of Shakespeare, ridiculing Derwinski's attempt to trot out the bard as justifier of Agnew's ethnic gaucherie. The general public, unfortunately, was uninterested in the Derwinski-Reuss exchange. Agnew was elected vice president, where he remained until his earlier bribe taking while governor of Maryland forced him to resign.

This was not my only attempt to use Shakespeare in politics. Back in 1964 George Wallace had brought his racist message to the Wisconsin Democratic presidential primary, where he was soundly defeated. Recalling Shakespeare's "What a lovely outside falsehood hath!" I proclaimed of Wallace, "We saw the inside of his outside — and we booted his backside back to Alabama!"

Another resort to the bard occurred when certain Republican members of Congress began calling the Democratic Party, with a snarl of disdain, the "Democrat Party." After enduring this for a time, I threatened that if they didn't stop, I would start calling them the "Publican Party." Publicans, of course, were the detested tax collectors of whom Shakespeare said, "How like a fawning publican he looks!" If they could drop a suffix from our name, we could drop a prefix from theirs.

7. See "Toward a Concert of the Democracies," which I wrote with former ambassador John W. Tuthill, in the fall 1994 issue of *Mediterranean Quarterly*.

CHAPTER 5. THE ENVIRONMENT

1. Ann Vileisis, in her *Discovering the Unknown Landscape: A History of America's Wetlands* (Washington, D.C.: Island Press, 1997), pp. 264–49, discusses Gilbert Swamp:

The Reuss subcommittee hearings provided an opportunity for supporters and opponents of channelization to air a broad array of opinions, experience, and information. As of 1971, SCS had spent an estimated $90 million channelizing six thousand miles of waterways; one thousand projects were in the works; and another two thousand applications awaited their rubber stamps. . . . Proponents claimed that the Small Watershed Program represented democracy at its finest: local soil and water conservation districts decided on projects they needed for flood control and other purposes, and then the SCS simply furnished technical expertise and helped to line up federal funding. Vice President of the National Association of Conservation Districts (NACD) George Bagley praised the grassroots aspect of the SCS program and made the zealous claim that in his community [it] "made it possible for the people to have shoes to wear, schools to go to, and churches in which to worship." The SCS's Small Watershed Program proudly took credit for building forty-nine public water supply reservoirs, for preventing $142 million of flood damages, and for providing over fifty thousand new jobs. SCS Assistant Deputy Administrator Eugene Buie declared that "American agriculture couldn't survive without it." Resting on its dust-bowl-era conservation laurels, the SCS further claimed that its projects always took fish and wildlife concerns into account and oftentimes even enhanced habitat.

Conservationists countered that projects were not actually initiated by small communities, but that the NACDs—backed by local development and construction interests—proposed projects to get the ball rolling. They contended that the SCS routinely exaggerated benefit estimates for recreation and flood control but underestimated lost recreational opportunities, lost flood-control benefits, and lost fish and wildlife habitat. Only through this fiscal sleight of hand could the destructive projects be approved and funded. Following ecological principles rather than engineering ones, conservationists preferred the more complex biological systems embodied by natural swamps and rivers to the SCS "improved" streams.

Bureau of Sport Fisheries and Wildlife studies backed up the conservationists' contentions. In testimony to the House oversight committee, Assistant Secretary of the Interior for Fish, Wildlife, and Parks Nathaniel P. Reed explained that reports compiled from Montana, Missouri, Florida, North Carolina, and Mississippi revealed that channelization reduced local populations of fish, vegetation, and ducks by 80 to 99 percent. Reed contended that if the SCS completed all 1,119 watershed projects planned for southern states, up to 300,000 acres of forested habitat—much of it bottomland hardwood forest—would be lost. "Stream channel alteration under the banner of 'improvement,' " he warned, "is undoubtedly one of the most destructive water management practices." In the ultimate insult to the SCS, Reed called the agency's program "the aquatic version of the dust-bowl disaster."

2. Wisconsin Academy of Arts, Sciences and Letters, "Report of the Kettle Moraine Task Force," *Wisconsin Academy Review* 42, no. 3 (Summer 1996): 44–49.

CHAPTER 6. FULL EMPLOYMENT WITHOUT INFLATION

1. In 1957 Ike proposed a modestly progressive budget and then repudiated it a month later at the behest of his ultraconservative treasury secretary, George Humphrey. I took to the House floor to brag about my solid record of supporting

Ike. The Republican side cheered, but that ended when I claimed, "I have a better record of Ike support than Ike does!"

2. Henry S. Reuss, *The Critical Decade* (New York: McGraw-Hill, 1964), pp. 172–74.

3. See my article, "How to Create 1 Million Jobs Without Swelling the Deficit," *Economic Policy* (1994), published by Committee for Developing American Capitalism, Bridgeport, Conn.

4. Tyler Bridges, *People and Taxes,* January 1983, pp. 1–8.

CHAPTER 7. INTERNATIONAL ECONOMICS

1. Cost-push inflation is that caused not by overall excess demand but by supply-side pressures like wage hikes or oil price increases.

2. This was Hubert's last trip abroad before his death in 1978, and he was at his best. We rode the Moscow subway while he worked it as if it were the Minnesota State Fair. At the huge white-tiled farmers' market where farmers from all over bring their onions and apples and peaches and turnips, a little old lady from Uzbekistan approached us, offered us an apple as wrinkled as she, and spoke the word that was totally appropriate: "Roosevelt."

In our afternoon-long meeting in the Kremlin with Premier Andrei Kosygin, we inquired about relative wages in the Soviet Union—say, a coal miner and a high-ranking bureaucrat. "Oh," said our host, "the ratio is about two for the bureaucrat to one for the miner." Interested, we asked the same question a few days later of our host in Warsaw, the distinguished physician who was president of the Polish Medical Society: how did *his* remuneration compare with that of a Polish coal miner? Same answer: about 2 to 1. But then it turned out that the coal miner was the 2 and the physician the 1.

3. Frank A. Aukofer, "Picks and Dollars Build Andes Road," *Milwaukee Journal,* March 21, 1978, pt. 1, pp. 11, 22.

CHAPTER 8. THE HOUSE BANKING COMMITTEE

1. Until then I had not prayed since as a five-year-old I had knelt at my sleeping-porch bedside early one August morning in 1917 to pray to God to return my lost wire-haired fox terrier, Brockie, not heard from for several days. As I prayed, Brockie appeared from nowhere and began licking the soles of my feet. At that moment my father, on his way to the bathroom, inquired what I was doing. I found this deeply embarrassing and refrained from prayer for several decades.

Having been baptized, confirmed, and married as a Christian, I have not been tempted to switch to Hinduism, Buddhism, Islam, or atheism. It was my good fortune to have available to me a faith based on the Old Testament's Isaiah—"For what does the lord thy God ask of thee, than to do justice, love mercy, and walk humbly before thy God?"—Christ's Sermon on the Mount, and the Apostle Paul's "I have fought the good fight, I have stayed the course, I have kept the faith."

My mentor in the House prayer group was Rep. Brooks Hays, Democrat of Little Rock. An admirable Christian (he was of the Campbellite sect), Brooks had a stock of stories that were truly parables. He lost his seat to the racism of the day in 1958, after he courageously defended the right of black students to attend Little Rock's Central High School. His autobiography, *Politics Is My Parish*, should be read.

2. Andrew Albert, "Henry Reuss Says Banks Fared Well During His Chairmanship," *American Banker*, January 6, 1983, pp. 2, 15.

3. James Galbraith and Henry S. Reuss, "The Fed's Inflation Fixation," *New York Times*, June 2, 1996, sec. 3, p. 12.

CHAPTER 9. THE CITY

1. See Henry S. Reuss, "Summary," *To Save a City* (Washington, D.C.: Public Affairs Press, 1977), pp. 1–5.

2. Committee on the Constitutional System, *Report and Recommendations of the Committee on the Constitutional System: A Bicentennial Analysis of the American Political Structure*, January 1987, Washington, D.C., p. 17.

3. The windmill duplicated one I had erected in 1975 out at North Lake in Waukesha County. The OPEC price hike had spurred efforts to develop new sources of energy that would not be dependent on the whims of the oil cartel. The genius behind our wind experiment was young Hans Meyer, son of the architect Mike Meyer, who had been my partner in the Red Arrow housing project of thirty years before (see Chapter 3). Hans's contraption was a souped-up version of a 1930s farm windmill. Its turbine generated electricity, which passed through a "synchronous inverter." This gadget harmonized its output with the electricity being supplied by Wisconsin Electric Power Company.

The end result was a system that satisfied our household needs for electricity when the wind was blowing, that took juice from the utility when the wind ceased to blow, and—best of all—fed surplus power into the utility grid when our windmill produced more electricity than we needed. This last feature—making the utility pay us as the meter needle moved backward—really captivated your average long-suffering utility customer.

True: the amount of electricity our windmill generated was not great. Bill Miller, the chairman of the Federal Reserve Board, came to Milwaukee to make a speech at my 1976 birthday dinner and acidly observed that the electricity we were producing was just sufficient to reverse the meter's needle. But the spirit was there. Wind power as a means of meeting part of the nation's energy needs continues to progress. In many areas it is economical right now.

CHAPTER 10. EQUAL RIGHTS

1. Miles McMillan, "Hello, Wisconsin," *Capital Times*, April 24, 1967, p. 3.

2. "By Valor and Arms," editorial, *Washington Post*, August 13, 1965, p. 16.

CHAPTER 11. SERVING CONSTITUENTS

1. Henry S. Reuss, "An Ombudsman for America," *New York Times Magazine*, September 13, 1964, pp. 30, 134–35.

CHAPTER 12. OUR CONSTITUTIONAL SYSTEM

1. Committee on the Constitutional System, *Report and Recommendations of the Committee on the Constitutional System: A Bicentennial Analysis of the American Political Structure,* January 1987, Washington, D.C., p. 18.

2. Ibid., pp. 10–11.

3. Kenneth L. Woodward and Jeff B. Copeland, "King or Country?" *Newsweek,* September 8, 1975, p. 65.

4. Twentieth Century Fund, *A Heartbeat Away,* with comments by Hugh Heclo, Henry S. Reuss, and Arthur M. Schlesinger, Jr. (New York: Twentieth Century Fund, 1986), pp. 17–18.

CHAPTER 14. REFLECTIONS ON THE GOLDEN AGE

1. This listing of values has many antecedents, going at least as far back as the 1339 fresco by Ambrogio Lorenzetti in the Town Hall of Siena. The fresco glorifies the civic virtues of prudence, faith, charity, peace, and magnanimity.

Index